Apple

iPhone SE
SENIORS GUIDE

Empowering Seniors to Master Their iPhone
with Confidence and Ease

- **LARGE ILLUSTRATIONS**
- **ACCESSIBILITY**
- **SIRI/SOS 911**
- **SETTINGS**
- **SOCIAL MEDIA**
- **HEALTH APPS AND MORE!**

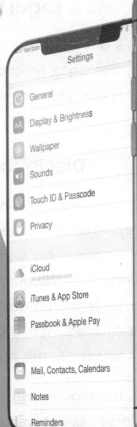

BRAD JORDAN

Copyright 2024 - All rights reserved.

Run a short team session and get everyone involved in identifying core values which represent the culture of the team 'the way we do things around here', emphasising the values and ethos of the way they work, what they value and how they value each other and their clients/ customers.

Legal Notice:

Disclaimer Notice:

TABLE OF CONTENTS

INTRODUCTION

While the iPhone SE was not specifically made for the seniors, it also has functionalities that suit them. It is possible to adjust some of the settings on the iPhone SE, and this aids some level of flexibility that accommodates people of all ages. This also contributes to narrowing the technological gap that exists between younger people and senior citizens. Besides, the iPhone SE offers all the advantages that an Apple smartphone can offer. If you are considering getting yourself an iPhone SE, or if you already have one, this guide will take you through all the basics that will enable you to enjoy your gadget.

Did you know that the total number of active iPhone users globally in 2022 is around 1.5 billion (Ruby, 2022)? Such large numbers of active users could be associated with the many advantages that come with iPhones, including the iPhone SE. As a senior citizen, there is no need for you to be left behind. Join in the wave and enjoy the technology together with your children, grandchildren, friends, relatives, and other people who matter in your life.

As it is said, "Knowledge is power," you can never understand how easy using an iPhone SE can be, unless you get the information somehow. In this case, this guide is a one stop information reservoir that will save you the hassle of gathering pieces of knowledge from the internet. Here are some interesting facts that iPhone SE for seniors:

- Although the home screen may have various applications, that should not demotivate you because most of the apps can be removed. This will help you to do away with unnecessary distractions that might make your experience with the iPhone SE appear more complicated, especially during the first days of using it.

- If eyesight is an issue, there's no need to worry. The iPhone SE has the features for zooming in and out, as well as adjusting the text size.

- Accessibility features such as the option to adjust hearing aids are also available for your convenience on the iPhone SE.

- If you are scared that your grandchildren might throw your gadget in water, the innovators of the iPhone SE also had you in mind when they developed this device. The iPhone SE has water-resistance properties that enable it to survive in onemeter depths of water.

- The iPhone SE comes with software support that spans up to seven years. That's long enough to make it easier for you to stick to your phone without any reason to change it, especially when you have become acquainted with how it works. Therefore, if you don't want to buy a new phone frequently, an iPhone SE is one of the options that you should consider.

- The iPhone SE has a touch fingerprint ID button that is big, so you won't struggle with unlocking the phone, as well as payment and banking applications.

- If you don't want to deal with the struggle of having to use cables when charging your phone, the iPhone SE has wireless charging functionality.

From these facts, you can see that there's no reason to hide from the iPhone SE your children bought for you, just because you think it is so complicated. In fact, by the time you get to the end of this book, you will be knowledgeable about various aspects, including connecting to the internet, as well as sending and receiving emails. Clear steps for completing various tasks on your phone are well-described and explained when necessary. This guide is presented in a manner that is easy to follow and understand, so you can even go through it on your own. Read on and operate your iPhone SE like a pro!

Chapter 1: Getting Started With the iPhone SE

iPhone SE

Do you already have your iPhone SE or you are still yet to get one? Whatever the case might be, learning how to get started with your gadget is one of the important first steps. In this chapter, we will take you through clear steps that you should follow as you enjoy your iPhone. We will highlight how you can unbox, set, and customize your iPhone SE.

By the time you get to the end of this chapter, you shouldn't have any issues trying to understand the home screen of your gadget.

Easy Steps to Unbox and Set Up Your iPhone SE

You might be surprised to note that getting started with the iPhone SE isn't complicated after all. Here are the easy steps that you can follow:

Unwrapping Your iPhone SE

Remove the plastic wrap from the box and lift the lid. You will find your iPhone SE, a charging cable, power adapter, and a pair of earphones inside the box.

Charging Your Battery

Simply connect the charging cable to the power adapter, and then connect the latter to the power outlet. To ensure that your iPhone SE will have maximum battery life and performance, charge the battery until it is full before you use it for the first time. If you start using your iPhone SE without fully charging it, you may find that the battery drains quickly and will require you to charge it more frequently.

Charging Your Battery

Simply connect the charging cable to the power adapter, and then connect the latter to the power outlet. To ensure that your iPhone SE will have maximum battery life and performance, charge the battery until it is full before you use it for the first time. If you start using your iPhone SE without fully charging it, you may find that the battery drains quickly and will require you to charge it more frequently.

Powering Up Your iPhone SE

To turn on your iPhone SE, press and hold the power button (located on the right side of the gadget) until the Apple logo appears. Once the logo is visible, wait for a few seconds until your iPhone SE is ready for use.

Selecting Your Preferred Language and Region

Once your iPhone SE is ready for setup, it will give you a list of languages to choose from. Select the language that you prefer as the default language for your entire iPhone SE. The language that you choose will determine your keyboard layout and other important features such as Siri, dictation, and the App Store.

After selecting your preferred language, choose the country where you will be using your iPhone SE from. The region or country you choose will determine some of the settings of your iPhone, including the date and format, as well as the currency used in the App Store. If you choose the wrong region and language, you can rectify the mistake by going to **Settings,** then to **General. Select Language and Region,** prior to choosing your preferred language or region.

Installing Your Security System

On the screen, your iPhone SE will ask you to scan your face by positioning it on the screen. To successfully scan your face, move your face in a circular motion so that your iPhone SE can capture all the angles on your face.

You can use your Face ID to unlock your phone and verify purchases on applications, including the App store, Apple music, and more. To set up your Touch ID, place your thumb on the home screen button multiple times so that your iPhone SE can capture your finger print. This particular feature can also be used to unlock your iPhone SE and verify payments on applications such as the App store, Apple music, and more

Face ID and Touch ID may not work perfectly in certain conditions. For example, the Face ID may not work if you are wearing a mask, while Touch ID may not work if your fingers are dirty or wet. In this case, the best alternative is to use a passcode that you enter manually.

A passcode is a security feature that allows you to lock your iPhone SE and protect your personal information. After entering your Face ID and Touch ID, your iPhone SE will prompt you to create a passcode. You can choose a passcode of your choice but it has to be a six-digit numerical number that you will not forget. You can also customize your passcode setting by choosing other options such as letters, numbers, and symbols.

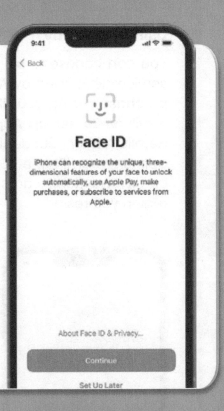

Exploring Settings

After completing the initial setup process your iPhone SE process will take you to the home screen where you can access various settings. In your settings, you can customize your iPhone SE according to your preference. These settings allow you to change settings such as wallpaper and screen time, as well as adjust the brightness of your screen.

The General Settings menu allows you to change settings such as accessibility options, background app refresh, software updates, and battery life. The General Settings menu allows you to customize various device settings, such as language and region, accessibility options, background app refresh, and software updates. Generally, settings allow you to customize your iPhone SE, based on how you want to interact with your phone

Using Apple Pay

You can choose to set up your Apple Pay, which is a payment service developed by Apple Inc. Apple Pay, allows you to make purchases using your iPhone SE at in-person stores and online retailers. To set up Apple Pay, you need to add your banking details (either your debit or credit card information) to the Wallet app on your iPhone SE. Apple Pay supports most of the major credit and debit cards issued by the banks in the country or region you reside.

To make a payment using Apple Pay, simply hold your iPhone SE near the store's contactless payment reader and authenticate using your Face ID, Touch ID, or passcode. Additionally, when making an online payment using Apple Pay, choose the Apple Pay option at checkout and you can authenticate using the Face ID or Touch ID verification method

Home Screen and Navigation

The home screen consists of application icons, folders, and widgets. The default home screen displays four docked icons at the bottom of your screen, which are visible on every page of different home screens. You can add more applications to your dock by pressing and holding the application icon until it starts to jiggle, then you can drag it out of the dock. Let's look at more ideas for navigating through the home screen:

Rearranging apps: To rearrange the apps on your home screen, press and hold an app until it starts to jiggle. Then, move the app to a new location on the screen. You can also move an app to a different home screen by dragging it to the left or right edge of the screen.

You can navigate between your home screen pages by swiping left or right on the screen. You can also skip to another page by tapping on the dots at the bottom of your screen. Another quick way to open your applications is by customizing your app icons using the Shortcuts app, which is pre-installed on your iPhone SE. With the **Shortcuts** app, you can create custom icons for your apps and add them to the home screen.

Customizing Your iPhone SE

If you want your iPhone SE to reflect your preferences through colors, designs, and other things, we are glad to let you know that you can customize these. Let's explore how you can do this in this section.

Choosing a Fresh New Look

The wallpaper is the background image on your iPhone SE's home and/or lock screen. Wallpapers give your iPhone SE a fresh and beautiful look. You can even make it feel personal. Follow these simple steps if you want to change your wallpaper:

Change the App Icons

1. Go to **Settings** on your iPhone SE.
2. Scroll down and tap **Wallpaper.**
3. Tap **Choose a New Wallpaper.**
4. Select an image from the pre-installed options or tap **All Photos** to select an image from your camera roll or gallery.
5. Tap **Set** to choose whether you want the image as your lock screen, home screen, or both

To change application icons on your iPhone SE, you can download a third-party application like an **Icon Theme** from the App Store. Open the application that you want to customize and select a new icon from the applications library or you can upload your own icon. Follow the instructions on the application to apply the new icon.

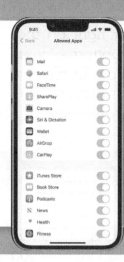

Enable or Disable Features

The iPhone SE comes with several features that you can enable or disable to better suityour needs or preferences. The steps below show how you can enable or disable features:

1. Go to **Settings** on your iPhone SE.
2. Scroll down and tap **General.**
3. Tap **Accessibility** to enable or disable features like AssistiveTouch, Zoom, or VoiceOver.

Customize the Control Center

You can customize the Control Center to add or remove shortcuts and rearrange the order of the shortcuts. Follow these steps to customize your Control Center:

1. Go to **Settings** on your iPhone SE.

2. Scroll down and tap **Control Center.**

3. Tap **Customize Controls** to add or remove shortcuts.

4. Tap and hold on to a shortcut to rearrange the order of the shortcuts

Change the Ringtone or Text Tone

Changing the ringtone or text tone is another way to customize your iPhone SE. You can choose from the pre-installed options or download new tones from the App Store. Changing your ringing tone or text tone can be done in the following few steps:

1. Go to **Settings** on your iPhone SE.

2. Scroll down and tap **Sounds & Haptics.**

3. Tap **Ringtone** or **Text Tone.**

4. Select an option from the pre-installed options or tap **Download All Purchased** Tones to download the ones you've purchased from the App Store.

Chapter 2:
Making Calls and Sending Message

One of the things that you are more likely to use your iPhone SE for is communicating with others. This involves making phone calls and sending direct text messages. This chapter has been compiled to make this form of communication easier when using your iPhone.

Making a Phone Call

You can make calls to contacts that are saved on your iPhone. Chapter 5 will take you through the steps involved when you are adding contacts on your gadget. You can also call people who are not in your contact list using the iPhone SE. Whether you are calling saved or unsaved numbers, here is how you can make a phone call:

1. Go to the **phone** icon on the home screen and tap on it.
2. Click **Keypad** for this tool to appear.
3. If the number that you intend to call is in your contact list, go to **Contacts.**
4. Scroll the contacts to get the one you want to call and tap on it.
5. **Tap on the number** that appears and make a call.
6. If the number you want to call is not in your contact list, write it using the keypad and tap to call.

Please note that you can hide the keypad by tapping Hide. If you want to put the call on hold for any reason, simply tap Mute and hold for five seconds. To resume your call, tap Hold once again. When you want to drop an ongoing call, tap End Call.

Sending a Text Message

To send a text message, follow these steps:

1. Go to **Messages** on the home screen.
2. You will see a **Compose** icon. Tap on it to create a new message.
3. Write the first few letters of the contact that you want to send a text message to. What you enter should match the saved name in your contact list. Select your preferred contact in the displayed list and then tap on the number that appears.
4. If the number that you want to send a message to is not in your **contact list,** first tap "123." After that, you can enter the number.
5. Go to the **text entry field** and tap on it.
6. Write your message.
7. Press **send.**
8. Go back to the home screen by tapping the **Home key.**

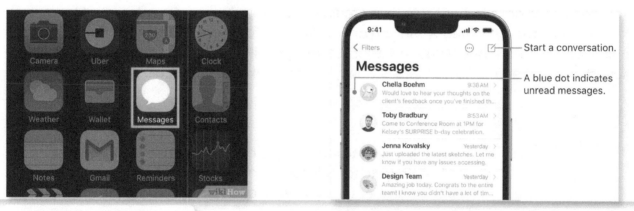

Start a conversation.

A blue dot indicates unread messages.

More Tips

If your effort to send a message is not successful, you will see an exclamation mark on it. You can try to resend the message by pressing Try again. Please note that the steps that we described above give you the basics for sending a text message using an iPhone SE. There are other thing that you might want to do, for example:

- **Reacting to a specific message that you received:** To do so, tap and hold the message. Various symbols for different reactions will pop up. Select the one that you want.

- **Forwarding a message:** Choose the message and press **More.** Highlight the relevant **messages Forward** icon. Select a **saved contact** or enter an **unsaved phone number** of the person you want to send the message to. Press the **send** icon.

- **Deleting messages:** Select the desired message and hold. Highlight the **messages** that you want to delete, before tapping on the **Delete icon.** You can choose Delete All if you want to get rid of all the text messages. Finally, tap the prompt that says **Delete message**

- **Deleting entire conversations:** Select the **message thread** that you want to delete.
- Drag the thread to the left. Tap on **Delete.**

  Pinning message threads: Go to the Message screen and choose the **message thread** that you want to pin. **Click Pin.** Please note that you can reverse the action,
- select the pinned **message thread and then tap Unpin.**

  Scheduling sending messages: While you are on the home screen, **choose short-cuts.** Go to the **Automation tab** and choose **Create Personal Automation.** Tap on **Time of the day** and then go to Time. Follow the prompts as you edit the time to your preference. Tap on Next. You have the option to choose how often you would want the message to be sent by **selecting Frequency.** Tap Next before clicking Send Message. From there, enter your text in the **message field.** Enter the **recipients**, select Done, and then **Next.** Tap on **Done** again. Having done this, your message will be automatically sent to the recipients at the time(s) that you designated

Using FaceTime to Make Video Calls

Video calling is gaining a lot of popularity, especially after the national lockdowns that were a result of the COVID-19 pandemic. This technology has made distance less of a barrier as people can still communicate while seeing each other in real-time on devices. FaceTime is one of the video calling tools that are currently used by many. Your grandchildren might want to show you their smiles, despite where they are, and Facetime can make that happen without you having to travel to them.

Here is how you can make a new video call with FaceTime:

1. Click on the **FaceTime icon** on your iPhone SE.

2. Select New **FaceTime**.

3. Type in the name, number, or email address of the contact you wish to FaceTime with. If you intend to FaceTime with more than one person in a call, just keep adding more contacts.

4. You have the leverage to choose between the Audio and FaceTime video. In this case, you will have to select **FaceTime video** to start the call.

More Tips

Sometimes turning off the video improves connectivity, as well as the quality of the call. Let's suppose that you have started a FaceTime video call, or answered one, here is how you can turn off the video:

1. As the call progresses, you will see a floating toolbar. Tap the **Camera** toggle on the toolbar.
2. You tap the same icon when you want to resume the video.

Let's also suppose that you are on a FaceTime call and you have something else that you want to attend to that is not in connection with the call, you could mute yourself. This way, people on the call won't be disturbed as they won't hear anything from your end. To mute yourself, simply tap on the **Microphone** toggle that appears on the floating bar on the call in progress.

Using Voicemail

Voicemail is a functionality that allows you to send and receive recorded audios as messages, like your old answering machine. When you receive voicemail messages, you always get notifications to alert you of a waiting message. Voicemail is an advantage when people fail to get in touch with you via calls due to issues such poor connectivity or if your phone has switched off.

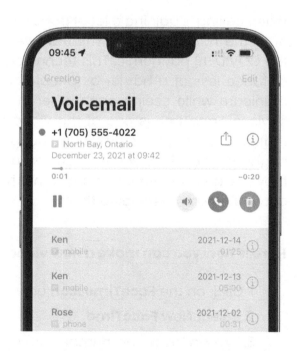

Setting Up Voicemail

To receive voicemail messages, you should go through the following set up steps:

1. Tap on the **Phone** app on your home screen.
2. Choose **Voicemail.**
3. Click on **Set Up Now.**
4. Enter a voicemail password, which has between 7 and 15 digits. **Tap Done.**
5. You will be prompted to re-enter the password. After that, press **Done.**
6. You have the option to use the default greeting by tapping **Default**. Alternatively, you can customize your greeting by choosing **Custom. Tap Done.**
7. After this, you will see your visual voicemail displayed on the screen of your iPhone.

An alternative way for setting up your voicemail would be by:

1. Tapping **Phone.**
2. Pressing the 1-key for longer.
3. Enter the voicemail password, in response to prompts.
4. Continue to follow the prompts on your phone.

Accessing Voicemail

Once you have set up voicemail, you can receive the recorded audio messages. Here is an outline of a few steps that you should follow to access your messages:

1. Click the **Voicemail i**con on your iPhone SE. Another option could be to select the **Phone icon** on the home screen, before going to **Voicemail**. This will lead you to your voicemail
messages.
2. To open and listen to voicemail messages that are tagged as "New," click only once. To enable playback for older voicemail messages, tap twice.
3. If you want to pause the voicemail message that you were listening to, tap on it once. It will stop. To continue listening from where you left, just click on the messages once again.
4. If you prefer to listen to your messages through the iPhone's speakers, just select the **Speaker** icon.
5. To get rid of messages that you no longer want, **select Delete.**

Answering Voicemail

Literally, every voicemail message on your iPhone is a sign that you missed some calls. It will be polite for you to respond to these messages if you don't prefer calling them back. You have the option to respond using the **"Reply with message" functionality.**

To activate the **Reply with message** option, swipe the phone button when a call is in progress. Once you do that, you will be presented with two options, which are "reply with message" or "remind me later." When you choose "reply with message," you are given these four options:

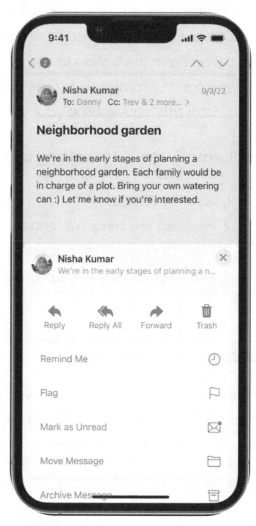

- What's up?
- I'm on my way.
- I'll call you later.
- Custom

With the first three options, you use them as they are. The last option gives you theleverage to create your own response that is personalized.

Chapter 3: Using the Camera

The iPhone SE has remarkable camera settings that allow you to capture stunning photosand videos. This chapter will equip you with knowledge on how to use your iPhone SE to take videos and photos. In some cases, you may want to edit your videos and photos. This chapter will provide the necessary information that will allow you to do so. After editing, perhaps you might want to share your videos and photos with loved ones. Be sure to go through this chapter to know how to share the contents of your library.

Taking Photos and Videos

When you open the **Camera** app on your iPhone, the standard mode that appears is that of **Photos**. You can use this mode to take live and still photos. To take live photos, using your iPhone SE, go to the Camera app and enable it by tapping on the Live **Photos icon**. Now, you can capture as many as you want

To use other **camera** modes, swipe right or left. The other camera modes include those of recording slow-motion, cinematic, and time-lapse videos. Under the options, you could lso choose to capture **photos** that have a square ratio or ones that are panoramic. Please note that if you like to save a certain mode as your default, you can change it using the **Save camera settings option.**

Launching the Camera Using Siri

You do not always have to employ the traditional route to use your camera. Instead of clicking on the Camera app, you could simply call on Siri to open the camera app and start taking photos. If you desire to capture videos, you can invoke Siri to launch the app, switch to video mode, and start recording

Using Photographic Styles

If you desire to personalize the appearance of your photos, you could employ photographic styles. These styles **include cool, warm, vibrant,** and rich contrast. Upon applying a certain style, the camera simply snaps photos according to your desired style.

1. To apply photographic styles on your iPhone, open the **Camera** app.

2. Choose the **Photo mode** on the horizontal menu under the viewfinder.

3. Afterward, select Photographic styles by swiping up from the underside of the view-finder. The icon of the **Photographic styles** appears like three cards arranged in a row.

4. Next, choose your desired style. You can fine-tune the appearance of your photos by using the **Warmth and Tone slider** that are below the viewfinder.

5. When satisfied, go on and click on the **Shutter** button.

Capturing Portrait Photos

In case you want to capture photos in portrait mode, the iPhone SE has an option to consider. Another outstanding feature of the iPhone SE is that it allows you to keep focus of your subject while manipulating the background so that it appears beautifully blurred

To capture portrait photos:

1. Open the Camera app and select the Portrait mode.

2. Next, use the yellow portrait box to put a frame on your subject. Afterward, drag the small box in order to choose a lighting effect. The lighting effects that you could choose from include the Studio, Natural, Stage, Contour, and high-Key Light Mono.

3. Once you are done selecting your effect of choice, capture the shot by hitting the Shutter button.

Editing Photos and Videos

It is possible to edit your videos and photos using iPhone SE. The editing tools are amazing in that they allow you to make changes to your videos and photos with excellent precision.In addition, it offers you some filters that help to beautify your shots. With these features, there is no longer need for an additional video editor app.

Update Your Software

Before you start the editing process, it is important that you update your software. To do the update, go to the Settings app, tap on General, and then Software Update.

Make Another Copy of Your Photo Before Editing

Please note that when you edit your photo, the old image is substituted by the edited one. However, it is important to note that you can undo the edits and go back to the original image at any instant. Sometimes you may want to keep both the original and edited versions though. Therefore, if you desire to keep both, it is advisable that you make a copy of the photo that you wish to edit.

1. To make another copy of an image, open the **Photos app, then picture.** At the bottom left, tap on the **Share** icon.

2. Afterward, scroll down and hit on **Duplicate.** When you go back to your photo library by tapping the **Back** arrow, you will see the copy of the image at the bottom. You can then make some changes to this one while the old one remains unedited.

3. To edit, click on the **Photos** icon and open the video or photo that you would like to make changes to.

4. Go to the top right and tap on **Edit.**

5. Depending on what you want to do, tap the bottom screen buttons to fine-tune **lighting, rotate, crop,** or *filter* your photo or video

Saving Your Edited Photo

When you finish making changes to your photo, tap on *Done* so that you can save the edits. Your edited picture will be in the photo library. In case you do not want to keep your edits, tap **Cancel,** then *Discard Changes* on your image in the Photo editor.

Sharing Photos and Videos

There are a number of ways that you could use to share videos and p`hotos on iPhone SE. These could be through other apps that you can install, **Messages,** or**Mail.** A remarkable feature of the iPhone SE is that it can choose your best photos from a certain event and recommend potential people to share them with.

1. In case you desire to **share** one video or photo, open it and tap the Share icon to
choose a command that allows others to have access to it.
2. Sometimes, you may wish to send several videos or photos. If you are looking at a screen with many thumbnails, click on **Select** before tapping on the photos and videos you would like to share. Tap the **Share** icon and choose how to share.
3. If sharing photos and videos from a particular **month or day,** tap on the **Library** icon, then on **Months or Days.** Afterward, tap on the **Three dots,** prior to tapping on the **Share Photos** icon. Select a share option.

Sharing Using iCloud

You can share numerous high-quality photos when **iCloud Photos** is turned on. All you need to access the videos or photos is a link. This link can be used to view photos and videos in the Mail or Messages app. Please take note that the iCloud links are only valid for 30 days.

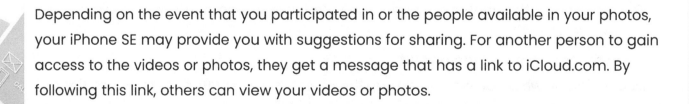

Depending on the event that you participated in or the people available in your photos, your iPhone SE may provide you with suggestions for sharing. For another person to gain access to the videos or photos, they get a message that has a link to iCloud.com. By following this link, others can view your videos or photos.

1. To share photos, tap **For You** prior to tapping a photo collection under **Sharing Suggestions.**
2. Afterward, tap **Next,** then **Share in Messages.**
3. You can then tap a suggested contact or **Add People** if you wish for more individuals to get the photos.
4. Last, tap the **upward-pointing arrow.** Upon sharing your photos, the recipients can also get prompts to share theirs with you. This usually happens if you were at the same event.

In case you wish to remove some items from Sharing Suggestions, tap them, then the **Three-dot i**con. Last tap on **Remove Sharing Suggestion.** If you need to revoke an already shared link, tap on **For You,** followed by the items under **iCloud Links.** Afterward, tap the **Three-dot icon,** then **Stop Sharing.**

Deleting Shared Album Videos and Photos

You can delete videos or photos from anyone that you may have shared your album with, just as long as you are the owner. Anything that you remove from the album gets automatically deleted, even on the other devices that you earlier shared with. However, if you downloaded a shared album to your **Photos library,** you remain with your videos or photos when they get deleted from the shared collection. In case the person who created the album stops sharing, your pictures or videos are safe if you had download-ed them in your Photos library.

To delete items from a shared album, open it and tap the photo or video. **Tap the Trash button** and **Delete Photo.**

Adding Videos and Photos to a Shared Album

It is possible to add more photos or videos to an album that you shared already. In the event that you added more items, the people who share the album with you receive notifications automatically. Remember to keep your **Subscribers Can Post** button turned on so that others can also add more videos or photos.

1. To add more photos to a shared album, open it and tap the **Add** button. Afterward, choose the videos or photos to add.
2. Alternatively, go to the **Library** tab and tap **Select** before choosing the photos or videos to add.
3. Afterward, tap the **Share** icon, then **Add to Shared Album**.
4. Next, select the album where you intend to send the items, then tap **Post.**

Sharing or Saving a Photo or Video That You Received

Whether you received photos or videos from a text message, email, or an iCloud link, you can also share them with others. If you are interested in keeping them, you could simply save them.

If you received a video or photos from email, tap to **Download,** then hit the **Sharing** icon. Alternatively, touch the item and keep holding it. Afterward, select a **Saving** or **Sharing** option.

In the case of a text message, go to the conversation and tap the **Sharing** icon. You should then choose a saving or sharing option. Another way to keep the received photos or videos in a **Messages** conversation is to tap the **Download** button. By tapping the Download button, the video or photos are directly saved to your Photos library.

If you received videos or photos from an iCloud link, tap the **Download** option to directly save the items to **your Photos** library. In case you are interested in sharing the collection of videos and **photos,** go to Photos and tap **For You,** then the group of pictures under **iCloud Links.** Tap on the **Three-dot icon,** then on **Share.**

File Types That Can Be Used in Shared Albums

When it comes to photos, the image formats that can be supported in the shared albums
of your iPhone SE include JPEG (Joint Photographic Experts Group), HEIF (High Efficiency Image File), TIFF (Tag Image File Format), RAW, PNG (Portable Network Graphic), and GIF (Graphics Interchange Format). In addition to these, special formats such as memory videos, live photos, slow-motion, and time-lapse can also be supported in shared albums. Please note that when in shared albums, photos can be reduced on the long edge to 2048 pixels. An exception is panoramic photos, which can reach a width of up to 5400 pixels. It is possible to share 100MB or smaller GIFs...
The video formats and file types that can be supported by shared albums include QuickTime, HEVC (High Efficiency Video Coding), MP4, MPEG-4 (Moving Picture Experts Group-version 4), and H.264. Videos can be up to 15 minutes long and they are delivered at a resolution of around 720p.

The Storage Limits of Shared Albums

The video formats and file types that can be supported by shared albums include QuickTime, HEVC (High Efficiency Video Coding), MP4, MPEG-4 (Moving Picture Experts Group-version 4), and H.264. Videos can be up to 15 minutes long and they are delivered at a resolution of around 720p.

Chapter 4:
Accessing the Internet and Mail

Smartphones are becoming less of a luxury and more of a requirement in today's connected world. Connecting to the Internet and using emails wherever we are, whenever we need to, is becoming increasingly crucial in our daily lives. You will need to connect to the internet to avoid missing important emails, stay current on the news, or even locate your way when you get lost. As much as your iPhone receives a strong mobile network signal, you can now access the internet at any location you are. Public Wi-Fi hotspots can also be used to establish a shared connection on the Internet. Once you are connected, you can now browse, send, and receive emails on your iPhone. This chapter will elaborate on the important steps that you should follow to access the internet and email, as well as browse the web

Connecting to Wi-Fi

Typically, there are two methods of connecting your iPhone to the web. The first method is through a digital cellular service provider or by using regular Wi-Fi. When the iPhone network connection is not very strong, a Wi-Fi-equipped gadget allows you to browse the Internet at free hotspots. Your iPhone can connect to the Internet by data transfer through a cellular service provider in a wireless link, much like what a computer does. There are two easy things you should do to connect to Wi-Fi. The first thing is to know the Wi-Fi name which can be referred to as a Service Set Identifier (SSID). The second thing is to know its password. Similar to other phones, you just need to add your iPhone to your Wi-Fi network once, unless you later change the password or network name. Let's go through some steps that you should take:

1. Start by tapping the **Settings** button that is displayed on your home screen.
2. Tap the **Wi-Fi** button to turn it on. Your iPhone will search for available Wi-Fi networks on its own.
3. To connect to a **Wi-Fi** network, tap its **username.**
4. A **padlock** icon will appear next to the network name when you are attempting to connect to a secure network. This indicates that you must provide a password before getting access to the Wi-Fi. Be sure you have the proper information before tapping **join** because failure to do so indicates that you entered the wrong password. If the password that you used previously doesn't work, it might be an indication that it has been changed.
5. Some hidden Wi-Fi networks will not instantly show up in the list of the provided ones. In that case, you should select **Other** (next to **Pick a network** option) if you are aware of the name network that is not appearing .
6. As you type the network's name, double-check your spelling and select Security.
7. Note that a network is not always safe just because it is concealed. If unsure, ask your network manager about the Wi-Fi network's security status.

8. To return to the previous screen and input the password in its field, click Other **Network.** To connect, click **Join.**

9. When you are now connected to the Wi-Fi, the upper left corner of the screen will display the icon and a tick next to the network's name

If you want to turn Wi-Fi off, go to the Settings page and click Airplane mode. An airplane will take the place of the Wi-Fi sign. By selecting Airplane mode once more, you activate Wi-Fi again.

Free Wi-Fi is now frequently accessible in many public locations, including airports, cafes, and college campuses, among others. Wired Access Points, which are needed to connect to Internet routers, are used to connect Wi-Fi (IEEE 802.11 standard) capable devices to the Internet. In essence, the access point is a Wi-Fi network arrangement that gives visitors access to the Internet. As Wi-Fi accesses a wired Local Area Network (LAN) extension, a user has more control over it. The LAN typically operates over short distances and may have a radio link or cable joining the access point to an ISP via routers. Wi-Fi is less affordable and uses a different wavelength than 3G.

Browsing the Web

On your iPhone SE, you will use the specialized search box to access Google or Yahoo! Please note that Google is the iPhone's default search engine. Let's go through the main steps you should take to browse using your iPhone:

1. From the center of the home screen, swipe downward.
2. Enter your search term after tapping the **Search** field. The things you have searched for will be displayed on the screen after a few seconds. Tap **Show More** or **Search** in the app to access additional results or conduct a search within anapp.
3. To view a search result, tap it.
4. If you want to search more, you have to open another tab by clicking the plus (+) sign on the right corner of your screen. Continue to type what you want to look for.

How to Browse Privately on Your iPhone

It's easy to have the ability to browse at any time, but you might prefer that your phone not save all of your web searches. For instance, you might not want others to get access to the history of your Internet searches if you routinely allow other people to use your phone. You can consider using the incognito mode, or private surfing, in this situation. This will enable you to visit websites without leaving any digital footprints on your iPhone. By setting up your iPhone to the incognito mode, you can feel more secure while browsing the internet because you won't have to worry about your browser history being stored on your device.

You can browse the internet in incognito mode without storing some information on the computer you are using. It ensures that there is no record of your search engine history, the websites you visited, or even your login information and associated passwords on that device. This feature is also known as the private browsing mode. Any cookies are deleted as quickly as you shut the incognito browser window, so none of these details are retained. Safari is the pre-installed browser for iPhones. Here's how to configure the incognito mode on your iPhone using Safari:

1. Launch **Safari.**
2. Just at the bottom right of the screen, touch the **tab** icon (it looks like two overlapping squares).
3. At the lower left corner of the screen, tap **private.**
4. Tap private once again to get out of **private** mode.

Once more, don't forget to close the private tabs on your browser when you finish browsing. By doing this, you can be sure that all of your device's cookies are removed and the secret session is securely concealed.

Using Email on Your iPhone SE

An email is a computer-based tool for message exchange between users. People can exchange emails quickly due to a global email network. The e-mail can offer benefits in flexibility and immediacy. An email is delivered to the targeted receiver's mailbox almost instantly, typically in the multiple-second to sub-minute range, unlike a traditional letter, which might take one day to a few weeks to arrive. This holds whether the emails are sent between friends who are located on different sides of the world or coworkers on the same floor of a company. Therefore, you will certainly need to use an email, especially if you want to communicate on a more professional basis.

How to Set Up an Email Account on Your iPhone

If you attempted adding an email manually to your iPhone but were unable, we are going to explain how you should go about it. To set up your iPhone email, simply follow the simple steps listed below:

1. Begin by going to **Settings** on your iPhone, then select **Mail.**
2. Tap on **Accounts** and then **Add** the mail account.
3. Select the **Apple Mail** and add it to your cell phone.
4. You will be requested to provide your email address and password for that service if you choose Google, Yahoo, or AOL. You can now create an email account with the service provider you've chosen.

How to Set Up an Email Account on Your iPhone

If you attempted adding an email manually to your iPhone but were unable, we are going to explain how you should go about it. To set up your iPhone email, simply follow the simple steps listed below:

How to Send an Email on iPhone

To send an email:

1. Go to the **email** app and click on it.
2. Your iPhone will display a screen with the emails you have already sent someone or, if you haven't used it before, you can click the **compose** button on the right side of your cell phone.
3. You will see a space named **"From,"** and this is where you should write your email you have created. The section named **"To"** is where you should put the name of your recipient. Enter the recipients names into the field after tapping it. **Mail** will provide contacts from your **Accounts** as you type, including email addresses for those contacts who have several email accounts. You may open Contacts by tapping the **Add Contact** button, where you can then add recipients.
4. The section with Cc is where you can also add other recipients who will also receive your email.
5. Tap the **Cc**/Bcc area, choose what you want to do, and then select the recipients you wish to send a copy. You can enter the recipients names in the Cc area after tapping it or the names of those whom you don't want to see in the **Bcc** box by clicking that field.
6. As soon as you've entered the recipients, you can rearrange their names in the address fields or move them to another such as the **Bcc,** if you think you may not want the names to show.
7. The section that is tagged **Subject** is where you should put the main aim of composing that email

8. You can proceed to write your email in the section that is written **Compose email.** If you want to attach a file, be sure to click at the far right corner of your iPhone. Your iPhone will display the command that you have clicked. It should display an **Attach File** prompt. You can retrieve the file from Google Drive or the internal storage of your iPhone. Follow the prompts on your iPhone until you have to click the document that you want to send.

9. If you wish to change your format, you can tap the **expand toolbar** on the top of your keyboard, then click the **format text** button. Adjust the font style and color of the text, add bold or italic text, and make a list with bullets or numbers, and more. If you have done that, you can now send your email by tapping the Send button.`

Receiving emails is straightforward. You wait until you hear a notification tone that shows that you have received an email message. When a message pops up, you will go straight to your mail and then click the message to read it. If you want to reply to the sender, you should click the **reply** button and start to text. A problem can arise when you are not receiving or able to send emails.

How to Rectify Email Problems

If you are experiencing problems sending emails using your iPhone's **Mail** app, there are a number of things you should think about and double-check. Also make sure your iPhone is connected to the internet. If you are still encountering problems, it is advised to seek help from an expert.

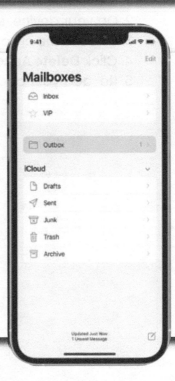

Check Your Outbox

Your Outbox will receive an email if you receive a notification stating that it was not sent. Follow this procedure to send the email once more after checking your Outbox:

1. Go to your list of mailboxes in **Mail.**
2. Click **Outbox.** If there is no Outbox visible, your email has already been sent.
3. In the Outbox, tap an **email.** Verify that the email address of the recipient is accurate.
4. Click **Submit.**

Get in Touch With the System Administrator or Your Email Provider

Contact your email provider or check their status page to see if there is a service interruption. Check with your email provider or system administrator to see whether you have set any security restrictions or limits for your email account, such as **two-step verification.** You might require a special password or authorization from your email provider in order to send and receive emails on your device.

Remove Your Account and Create Another One

Replacing your email with a new one involves the following steps:

1. Log in to your email provider's website on your computer. Check to see if anything you sent via email is there, or make sure it is saved elsewhere besides your iOS or iPhone device.
2. On your device, select **Settings, Mail,** and then click **Accounts.**
3. Choose the email account you wish to delete and tap it.
4. Click **Delete Account.**
5. Re-add your account using the steps that we described earlier.

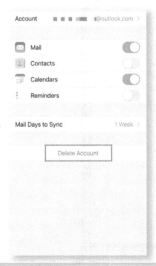

Chapter 5: Managing Your Contacts

The **Contacts** app is the oldest one of its kind and was introduced in 2007 when the first iPhone was launched (Bryant, 2020). The **Contacts** app is one of the most important applications on your iPhone. Upgrading is being done when necessary although a little has been changed up to date. This is an advantage to the seniors as they don't need to continue learning new things every time they use their phone. Once you are used to this app, there are no more challenges even if you buy a new version of the iPhone. As a senior,

you may think that managing your contacts on an iPhone SE can be a bit overwhelming. The process is an easy one, so don't hesitate to buy one for yourself and enjoy other benefits that come with it. In this chapter, you will learn more about how you can successfully

Adding Contacts

You can add as many contacts as you need on your iPhone and use them at any time. You can save phone numbers, email addresses, birthdays, and postal or physical addresses of anyone you know. The Contacts app is linked to your email account, which is iCloud for most iPhone users; but Microsoft Exchange, Gmail, and many others you know can work as well. So, you should have an email account added to your iPhone before saving contacts

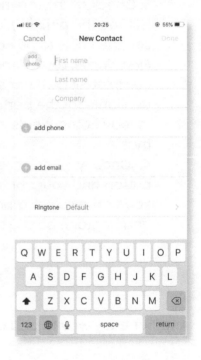

Setting up Contacts in Your Email Account

When adding your email account to your iPhone SE:

1. Look for Settings on your device's home screen. Tap on the Settings app and then scroll down until you see Passwords & Accounts.
2. Click Passwords & Accounts and then on the Add Account option. Once you tap on it, the list of all accounts will appear, so you should select the email account to use.
3. Tap your email account and toggle on Contacts. The toggle switch will turn green when on and white if it is off. So, you should see a green color on the switch when you toggle on Contacts. Now, your Contacts are contained in the email account.
4. If you don't want to use your email account, set up a contact account like CardDAV or LDAP.
5. Continue the process by tapping Other and entering your user information and password.
6. Then, tap Next to finish the process.

If you have many email accounts, you should centralize your contacts by setting up a default account. On iPhone SE, iCloud is mostly used as the default account. So, you can use it as well. To set the default account, go to your home screen and tap on the Settings app. Select the Contacts option, and then choose Default Account. Choose the account you want from the given list and your contacts will be added to it.

Steps to Add Contacts on Your iPhone SE

To add contacts to your device:

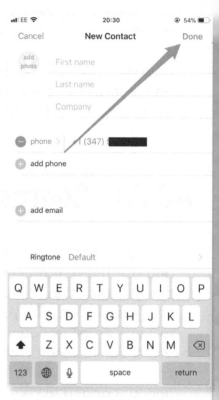

1. Go to the home screen and tap on the **Phone** icon.
2. Click on **Contacts.**
3. Check at the top-right corner of your screen, you will see the **plus** (+) icon. Tap on it so that you can see the fields to be completed like **Add Phone Number, First Name,** Last Name, and **Company.** You should complete where necessary according to the information available for the particular contact. So, it is possible to leave other fields incomplete and nothing is wrong with that.
4. Once you finish entering the details, Click the **Save** button and your contact will be added to the **Contacts** list. You can also set a personalized text tone, contact image, and ringtone before saving for ease of identification.

Another easy way to add contacts to your iPhone SE is as follows:

1. On the home screen, tap the **Phone** icon. The **Keypad** tab will appear, then type the phone number you want to add.
2. Check below the digits you entered, there will be an **Add Number** option. Click it and you will see options popping up.
3. Options like, **Create New Contact** and **Add to Existing Contact** will appear and you should choose one. If you select **Create New Contact,** you will automatically see the fields to enter the details. After entering the contact details, like names, you can now tap on the **Save** button. If you want to check whether it is saved or not, search for it by clicking on the **Phone** icon. On the upper part of the device, type the contact name you had just saved in the box written "**search contacts."** If the contact appears on the list, it shows that it has been saved. Make sure you write the same spelling as the saved one.

Organizing Your Contacts

Organizing contacts on your iPhone SE can be of great importance. It may assist you to keep track of your critical contacts for easy identification when you need to use them. There are many ways you can organize your contacts:

Use Nicknames

Add nicknames for your contacts so that searching for them can be easy. Nicknames can be added to contacts with longer names, or when there are many similar titles. This will save you time to type longer names when searching or from confusion in trying to figure out if it is the correct contact to dial or send a message to. For example, you have a friend called Budchad but you always call them Bud. So, you can add it to the Nickname field. You will type this short name and the contact will appear.

When adding a nickname:

1. Open the **Phone** app and choose the **Contacts** tab. The contacts will appear, then click on the one you want to add a nickname.
2. Then, tap **Edit** and **Add Field** option will appear. Click on it and you will see the fields on your screen.
3. Look for **Nickname** and enter the details there.
4. Then, click **Done** and your nickname is now saved

Add Pictures

You can also use profile pictures to quickly identify the exact person you want to communicate with. To add the picture:

1. Click the **Phone** app on the home screen.
2. Select the **Contacts** tab and all the contacts in the list will appear.
3. Choose the contact you wish to modify and then tap **Edit.**
4. Select the **Add Photo** option. The pictures can be images from the library, Emojis and Memojis, or you can take a photo if the person is with you. So, you should choose one and add it.
5. Tap **Done** and the photo is instantly uploaded to the profile. So, when searching for that contact, the profile picture will also appear.

Changing the Display and Sorting Order

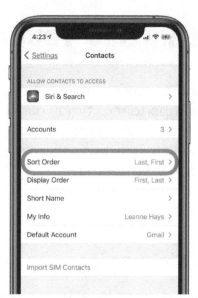

When adding contacts to your iPhone SE, they are automatically sorted in alphabetical order by their last names. This is the default setting but you can change this and arrange them using the first name

To change:

1. Go to the home screen and select **Settings** app.
2. Click **Contacts** and then tap **Sort Order**. The options to select from will appear. Then, select **First Name.** You can also click on **Display Order** so that you can change the way contacts are displayed. You can choose **Last Name First** or **First Name First.** The contacts will instantly change.

Use Favorites List

Frequently used contacts are usually found on the Recents tab. Sometimes it can be cluttered with many numbers that you have to scroll a long way to get the contact you want to use. You may not find the contacts in the Recents tab if you clear them. As a result, there will be a need to revisit the Contacts tab to search for it again. So, to lessen the burden, add the frequently used contacts to the Favorites list.

To add favorites:

1. Go to the **Contacts** app, find the **Recents** tab, and tap the **Information (i)** icon. You can also use the **Contacts** tab to select the desired number.
2. Tap **Add to Favorites** and then choose Call, **Video, or Message.**
3. Afterward, select the corresponding app like WhatsApp, Telegram, or Call (depending on the mode of communication you usually use most with the chosen contact).
4. Finally, your contact is added to the **Favorites** tab in the **Phone** app

Name Your Contacts According to How You Know the Person

You may have two contacts with the same name. It may be difficult to differentiate them when calling or receiving calls and messages from them. Naming them according to what they do can make your life easy. For example, you know a Peter from the golf club and another from college or an organization. So, to solve the problem, add the name of the school, club, or workplace of that person like this, Peter@Golf.

Merge or Remove Duplicate Contacts

Smart Cleaner can help you remove duplicate contacts.

1. Select Smart Cleaner's Contacts page.
2. Then, to view the duplicate contacts, select the Duplicates option. Tap on the contact to be erased from the list.
3. Click Edit and then tap on the Delete icon to erase the number you no longer need.

You can also merge the duplicate contacts to make one. In the Smart Cleaner app, choose the Duplicate Contacts page. Select the duplicates and tap Merge so that they instantly become one contact.

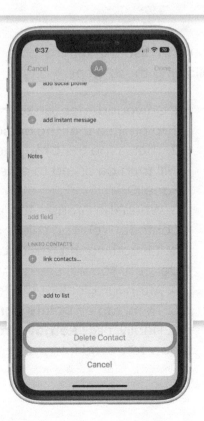

Deleting Contacts

Deleting contacts permanently from your device and email account is an easy task. Be sure you want to go through with the process before performing it so that you won't regret.

36

Deleting One Contact At A Time

If you want to delete the contact:

1. Open the **Contacts** tab and select the contact you would like to be removed.
2. Go ahead and tap **Edit,** then scroll down.
3. Using your finger, tap **Delete Contact.** This will bring up a confirmation message asking if you want to delete the contact.
4. Confirm that you want to delete the contact by tapping **Delete Contact** again. Once you do this, the contact is no longer on your list.

Deleting Multiple Contacts

You can also remove multiple contacts at one go using an easy-to-follow process. To do this:

1. Click on the **Contacts** app to open it and tap on the **Groups** button located in the upper-left corner of your device.
2. From there, select **All Contacts,** and you will see a list of all your contacts.
3. Tap **Select** in the top-right corner of your iPhone SE. Then, mark the phone numbers you want to remove.
4. Finally, tap **Delete** in the lower-left corner of the screen and confirm that you want to delete the selected contacts. The task is complete.

You can also use a third-party tool to erase multiple contacts from your device by following these steps:

1. On your device, go to the **App Store.** The search bar will appear on your screen. Tap on it so that the cursor will appear.
2. Then, type the **Groups** app and click the Get button to start searching for it. You will then be asked to enter the App Store passcode or to authenticate with your Face ID.
3. When the Groups App is installed, open it and make sure you allow it to read contacts. You can select contacts for the Group list. All contacts can be selected; but if you want a few to be included, tap on the left side of each contact name to be deleted. You will see a checkmark on every contact you selected.
4. Afterward, look at the top of the screen and tap on **Choose Action.**
5. Then, tap on **Delete Contacts** which will appear on the pop-up menu.
6. Finally, click **Remove from my iPhone** to delete the contacts. Your contacts are now removed from your device.

Restoring Deleted Contacts

If you accidentally delete contacts from your iPhone SE, don't panic as there are some ways to retrieve them. You can use an iCloud account or iTunes backup. To successfully recover them, you should have previously backed up your contacts to both the iTunes and iCloud account.

> If you are trying to retrieve them from an iCloud account:
> 1. Go to **Settings** and then **iCloud.**
> 2. Go on to select **Contacts** and turn on the toggle. Your contacts will start to sync to the iCloud account.
> 3. To complete the process, log in to your iCloud account on a computer to export and

How to Use the Magnifier App on Your iPhone

To use the magnifier app, go to the right-hand side of your iPhone's screen and swipe down. Afterward, tap the **Magnifier** icon. By doing this, the app will be launched and you should see the live view window on the screen's top. The different magnifier controls will appear at the bottom and you can select from these according to your preferences.

The Magnifier controls for iPhone include options that allow you to adjust your phone's brightness, color filters, zoom level, and many others. Let's look at them individually:

1. To adjust the brightness, tap on the sun-shaped button.

2. If you need to turn on the flashlight of your iPhone, just tap on the button that has the shape of a flashlight.

3. To switch your camera to the back or front, press on the camera icon that has arrows, then tap back or front.

4. You may wish to save a magnified item as an image. To do this, just press on the large freeze-frame button at the center. In case you want to share, do it by using the **Share** icon at the top right of your iPhone's screen.

5. To change the zoom level, simply drag the control slider to the right or left.

6. Tap on the filters button that has the appearance of a Venn diagram in order to affect color filters.

7. To fine-tune the contrast, tap on the two-tone circle contrast icon.

When using iTunes, connect your device to the computer. To continue, open **iTunes.** When you see the **Phone** icon, click on it. Then **Restore Backup** will appear. Click on the prompt and choose the backup that has your contacts

Chapter 6: Using Siri

You can think of Siri as a personal assistant who is always available to assist you in performing tasks on your iPhone SE. It is an interactive voice that helps to get the information that you need from your iPhone. Siri is based on the technology of voice recognition and artificial intelligence (AI). A survey that was done in 2021 showed that approximately 90% of people use Siri on their phones more than on other gadgets (Thormundsson, 2022). This probably shows how credible this tool is, and possibly even better on your iPhone SE. You are probably thinking, "How does that work?" There is no need to worry because this chapter will take you through all the basics that will make it easy for you to use Siri.

One of the main advantages that come with using Siri is that you can complete tasks relatively faster. Siri is an intelligent virtual assistant who is quite helpful when you have questions. This feature can even assist you with directions, making reservations, sending emails and text messages, and making recommendations where necessary. It is also possible to activate the low power mode on your iPhone using Siri

Another piece of good news is that Siri does not only use English. The virtual assistant can speak and understand other languages as well. This is a great functionality if you are not fluent in English or want to learn a new language. When you are all alone and feel bored, Siri can be a friend that keeps a smile on your face. Just ask Siri a funny question and this virtual assistant will get you laughing. So, you can use Siri to perform a range of tasks, from professional to personal ones. However, it is also vital that you note that Siri is not perfect, despite being extremely helpful. Having said this, let's get down to exploring how to use Siri and customize its settings.

Set Up Siri

Siri won't work on your iPhone unless the feature is activated. You can easily note that this tool is not working on your iPhone if you speak to Siri and don't receive a response. The set-up process will only take no more than three minutes of your time; and the best part is that it is so easy. Let's go through the steps that you can take to set up Siri before using it:

1. Go to your iPhone's home screen and access the **Settings**.
2. Scroll down the options for settings, and then press **Siri & Search.**
3. You will see a switch at the top of the screen that appears. Click on it so that it turns green. Enable **Listen for "Hey, Siri."**
4. You will be prompted to set up **"Hey, Siri."** Simply press **Continue.**
5. You will also be prompted to recite some phrases to your iPhone SE. This way, Siri will be calibrated. Moreover, the virtual assistant will get acquainted with your voice.
6. Press **Done.**

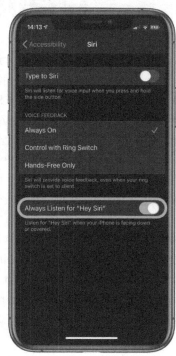

Accessing Siri

There are basically two ways through which you can access Siri:

- **Through your voice:** To access Siri, you could just say, **"Hey, Siri"** while projecting your voice to your iPhone. Try to be as clear as possible so that Siri can quickly pick up what you are saying and command the right task.

- **Through a button:** If you don't prefer accessing Siri using your voice, you can also do so through a few clicks. Simply go to your **iPhone settings,** and then to **Siri & Search**. Press **Listen for "Hey, Siri"** to access the **Press Home Button** for Siri. On your right, you will see a switch that you should press so that it turns green. Now, hold on to your home button and start communicating with Siri.

Start Using Siri

As is the case when you activate Siri, you can use this software through your voice and the home button. In this section, we will pose various examples that highlight how you can use this feature. The purpose of this is to make you understand the whole process as much as possible. Here are the steps involved when you are using Siri:

1. Open Siri by saying, **"Hey, Siri."** Alternatively, you can press and hold the **Home** button.

2. Let's suppose you want to send a text message to someone, say, **"Message."** Then,
tell Siri the name of the contact or their number. Finally, recite the message that you want to send. When you are done say, **"Send"** or click the **Send** button on your iPhone.

3. If you desire to make a direct phone call, simply say, **"Call."** Say the contact's name,
followed by their number. The number that you want to call will be automatically dialed and you get on with your call.

4. If you are looking for directions to a specific location, say, **"Directions to."** After this, say the specific location or recite the address. Just by doing this, the **Maps** app will open.

5. Do you often use alarms as reminders? If yes, you can also do this using Siri by saying, **"Set an alarm."** Tell Siri the time when the alarm should ring. The alarm
6. If you want to check up on the weather, start by stating the location. Say, **"Weather"** and the information that you are looking for will be displayed on your screen.

7. You can instruct Siri to search for your photos, starting by saying **"Photos."** Next, mention the subject that is associated with the photo. For instance, you could say, **"Photos for flowers."** The images that Siri finds will be shown on your screen.

8. To play your favorite songs, say **"Play"** and then specify the name of the song that you want. Alternatively, you can **name the artist** of the song and the music will start playing. Did you know that you can even let Siri help you to find the name of a song that is playing on your iPhone SE? Well, all you should do is say, **"What is this song?"** Siri will listen to the song, and you will see the song's details displayed on your iPhone SE's screen.

9. Are you often caught up with the need to make conversions between various units of measurement? If yes, just tell Siri the units of measurement that are involved in the conversion. For example, you can say. **"How many pounds in a kilogram?"** You will get the conversion on your screen.

10. If there is an app that you want to open and you don't want to go through the series of clicks, just say, **"Open"** and then name the app. The specified app will open on the screen of your iPhone.

11. Siri is also there for sports lovers. Find out the scores for your favorite sports by mentioning the team's name. The latest scores of the team that you mentioned as well as the games that are upcoming will be displayed on your iPhone's screen.

12. Add reminders by saying, **"Remind me to,"** and then mention the associated task. The reminder will be automatically set on your iPhone SE.

From the steps that we described in this section, you can possibly tell that there is a lot that you can do with Siri.

Customizing Siri Settings

Siri has default settings that you can change to your preferences. For instance, you could lock access to Siri when your phone is off. You can even change Siri's voice! This section has been compiled to help you to customize Siri settings so that they match your preferences.

Changing Settings on When Siri Should Respond

It's up to you to determine whether Siri should respond to the button press or your voice, and you can set that up in the settings. You can also set up your preferred language when you give Siri commands.

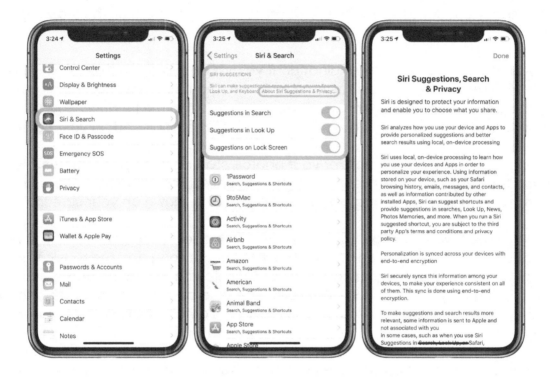

Go to **Settings** on your iPhone, press **Siri & Search,** before you can make changes to Siri settings as follows:

- If you don't want Siri to respond to voice commands, switch off **Listen for "Hey, Siri."**

- If you prefer using voice requests rather than the **Home** button, switch off the button settings.

- If you don't want Siri to be accessed when your iPhone SE is locked, simply switch off **Allow Siri When Locked.**

- To make changes to the language that Siri should respond to, go to **Language** and then select the language that you prefer

Changing Settings on How Siri Should Respond

There are mainly three options as to how Siri responds to your request; it could be silently, through a text on the screen, or loudly. You can also choose to have your commands appear on the screen or not. To start making changes on how Siri should respond, follow the steps described here:

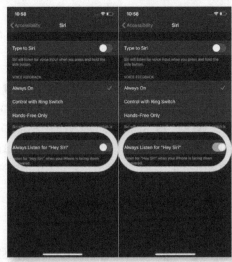

First, go to Settings, then to Siri & Search, prior to doing the following

1. If you want to see Siri's responses on screen, press **Siri Responses**. Switch on **Always Show Siri Captions.**

2. To change when Siri should give voice feedback, go to **Siri Responses,** and then to **Spoken Responses.** Make your choice among the available options that appear.

3. If you prefer that your request appears on screen, go to **Siri Responses.** Click on **Always Show Speech.**

Changing Siri's Voice

Please note that changing Siri's voice is an option that is not feasible for some languages. If your language is compatible with the functionality, follow these steps:

1. Click **Settings** and then go to **Siri & Search.**

2. Press **Siri Voice,** and then choose your preference among the available options.

Changing the Apps That Appear in Search

You can also decide on apps that should appear when you are using Siri by following these few simple steps:

1. After clicking **Settings,** press **Siri & Search.**

2. Scroll down on the available options and tap on the app whose settings you want to change.

3. Turn the settings of the app on or off, depending on whether you want it to appear or not.

Changing Settings on Accessibility Features

Accessibility features are easy to explore when you use Siri. To access these features using Siri, you can either say, **"Turn off VoiceOver"** or **"Turn on VoiceOver."** The Siri software determines whether Voiceover is on or off. VoiceOver is a functionality that you can use to read what is shown on your screen by Siri. Through VoiceOver, Siri can also read for you, though this virtual assistant sometimes provides you with more information than what you can see on the screen of your iPhone.

Changing Settings on Whether Siri Should Announce Settings

It is possible for Siri to announce notifications from various apps that include messages. Siri uses the iPhone speaker for this task. Whether you want this functionality on your iPhone or not, change your settings accordingly as described below:

1. Access **Settings** on your iPhone SE.

2. Press **Accessibility,** and then tap **Siri.**

3. If you want Siri to announce notifications, switch on **Announce Notifications on Speaker.**

4. Press **Announce Notifications.** You can then go to each app and determine whether Siri should announce all announcements or only those that are time sensitive.

Changing Siri Accessibility Settings

To make any changes to Siri accessibility settings, press Settings, and then go to Accessibility, before tapping Siri. Then:

If you would rather type than talk to Siri, click **Type to Siri** to switch this command on. Once this is done, you will only be able to make requests to Siri by typing in the text field.

You can control Siri's voice feedback. You can give Siri the leverage to determine when to speak by tapping on **Automatic,** under **Spoken Responses.**If you want Siri to speak whenever it's possible, regardless of whether the phone is on silent mode or not, tap **Prefer Spoken Responses.**

Troubleshooting Siri

If Siri seems not to be working on your phone, check a few settings that might need to be addressed. Here are some troubleshooting tips that you could try:

Is Hey Siri Turned On?

To check if Hey Siri is turned on:

1. Open **Settings** and go to **Siri & Search.**

2. Ensure that **Listen to "Hey Siri"** and **Allow Siri When Locked** are turned on

Listen for "Hey Siri"

Press Side Button for Siri

Allow Siri When Locked

Has Siri Stopped Responding?

If Siri is no longer responding:

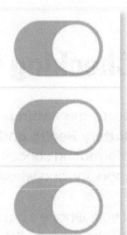

1. Open **Settings** and go to **Siri & Search,** then **Siri Responses.**
2. Select **Prefer Spoken Responses.**

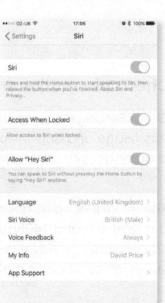

Chapter 7: Managing Your iPhone SE

Unlike other complex iPhone series, an iPhone SE is much simpler and suitable for use by the elderly. Besides other functions, it is good to know how you can check the health of your device. The iPhone has two ways that you can use to check the remaining battery power: the **battery percentage** and **battery level** icon.

If you are using the second-generation iPhone SE, you should go deep into the settings panel to know the exact battery percentage remaining. This generation of iPhone only shows the battery level icon, which gives you only a rough estimate of the remaining power.

Checking Battery Life

Go to the **Settings** panel and tap **Battery,** then open **Battery Health and Charging.** Your iPhone will display information concerning the battery's peak performance, capacity, and whether battery service is necessary.

If your iPhone's battery is not serviced timely, it can lead to malfunctions and slowperformance. By checking on the battery life, you can know when it is necessary to get itserviced or changed. Bear in mind that as time goes on an iPhone battery wears out, affecting its performance and capacity.

Check Information on Battery Usage

Go to **Settings** and open **Battery.** You will see details of battery usage and activity for the last 24 hours. Information about battery activity that can be displayed extends to the last 10

The initial iPhone SE device and the iPhone SE (2020) do not have big batteries. Their batteries are 1821mAh and 2406mAh in capacity respectively, which is quite low compared to the larger iPhone versions. However, these batteries have amazing endurance, which is made possible by super-efficient chips that are inserted by Apple, inside the most affordable versions

Managing battery usage on your iPhone remains one of the most important actions that you should execute regularly. This helps you to maintain and maximize the performance of your iPhone SE.

Insights and Suggestions

Battery
Battery Health
Phone batteries, like all rechargeable batteries, are consumable components that become less effective as they age. Learn more...
Maximum Capacity
100%
This is a measure of battery capacity relative to when it was new. Lower capacity may result in fewer hours of usage between charges.
Peak Performance Capability
Your battery is currently supporting normal peak performance.

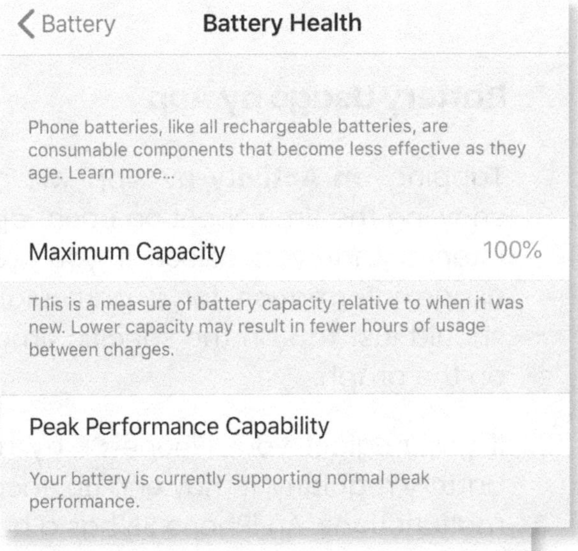

Insights concerning the usage patterns and conditions that lead to excessive consumption of energy may pop up here. Actions and suggestions that you should take to lower the consumption of energy may also appear. If such suggestions show up, you should tap on them to activate the corresponding setting.

Last Charged

If you tap on **Last Charged**, information about when the last full charging was done and the time of disconnection from the charger will be displayed.

The Battery Level Graph (in Last 24 Hours)

If you tap on **Battery Level Graph,** you will see the iPhone's battery level and intervals of charging. The period when the battery was low, or when the Low Power Mode was activated, is also shown here

Battery Usage Graph (in the Last 10 Days)

Taping this graph displays the battery power percentage consumed each day

Activity Graph

If you tap on the Activity Graph, you will see activity over a certain space of time. It also shows you whether the device's screen was active or off.

Screen On and Screen Off

When you tap Screen On and Screen Off, the device will show you the total battery activity for a certain time interval. It shows the details of when the device's screen was on and off. When you go to The Last 10 Days view, you will see the average power usage per day.

MESSAGE
CALL
SEND

Battery Usage by App

Tapping **on Activity** by App will display information showing the time spent on each app in a certain time interval that you select. If you want to see battery usage information for a particular day or hour, you should just tap on the specific time interval displayed on the graph.

If you neglect your iPhone SE by not checking on the battery regularly, it may end up encountering a series of malfunctions. An iPhone SE has a battery that gives you around 15 hours of continuous video playback. It also gives you a minimum of 10 hours of video streaming and around 50 hours of audio playing. However, due to the limited lifespan that the iPhone batteries have, regular checks on battery health and performance should be done.

Therefore, knowing the apps that drain your device's battery more is one of the most life saving actions you can take to help it last longer. Keep in mind that as the battery weakens
or ages, so does the iPhone's performance.

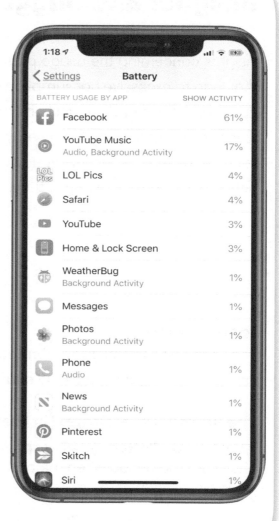

Updating Software

Just like all other iPhone versions, iPhone SE requires software updates. You simply have to make sure that you install the latest approved software versions. Installing unapproved versions, like the Beta versions, can come with issues like app activation problems and device malfunctioning.

iOS Update Using Wi-Fi

Follow these steps:

1. Go to the iPhone's home screen, and tap on the **Settings** icon.

2. Select **General** and navigate to **Software Update.**

3. If the device shows more than one update option, you should choose the one that you want.

4. If you see the **Download and Install** option, just tap it and the device will download and update the software.

5. If the device asks for your password, just enter it and tap **Install Now.**

6. You will be asked to review the **Terms and Conditions** and tap **Agree** to continue.

Once this is done, the iOS update begins and this process may need several minutes to be completed. Please note that you should not interrupt the process while it is still in progress.

Additionally, in some instances, a message requiring you to create more space for the update whilst it is still in progress may pop up. If you see this message, tap **Continue to** allow the highlighted apps to be temporarily removed. Once the installation is complete, the removed apps will be automatically reinstalled.

However, it is also possible to delete the apps and any other content manually. This can be done by tapping **Cancel** when the message appears. This action allows you to pick the apps that you would want to delete to free up the needed space.

Customizing Automatic Updates

Customizing your device to automatically update its software is ideal, especially for seniors who would not want to be bothered by software update issues.

How to Turn Automatic Updates on

1. Tap on the **Settings** icon, open **General,** and go to **Software Updates.**

2. Select **Automatic Updates,** and switch on **Download iOS Updates.**

3. Switch on **Install iOS Updates** and your iPhone SE will be ready to update to the latest iOS version automatically

Backing Up Your iPhone SE

There are two ways that you can backup your iPhone, and these are through the use ofiCloud or a computer. Backing up your information and files is important because you cansimply get them back when your device is lost or replace it. Without backup, you will risk losing all files that are on your device.

Backing Up iPhone SE Using iCloud

iCloud allows you to safely back up your files and have them back when you need them.

1. Go to the iPhone's main menu and open **Settings.**

2. Tap on your name and proceed to iCloud. Afterward, tap **iCloud Backup.**

3. Switch on **iCloud Backup.**

Each time your iPhone is locked, connected to power and Wi-Fi, iCloud will automatically back up your device. If your iPhone supports 5G, there may be an option to use a cellular network to backup your device.

Backup Using Cellular Network

Follow these steps:

1. Note that this option applies only to 5G-supporting devices.

2. Go to **Settings**, tap on your name, and proceed to **iCloud.**

3. Tap **iCloud Backup** and turn on **Backup Over Cellular.**

4. If you wish to perform the manual backup immediately, tap **Backup Now.**

Viewing iCloud Backups

It is possible to view the files that are backed up or stored on iCloud.

1. Just go to **Settings** and tap on your name.

2. Open **iCloud** and proceed to **Manage Account Storage.**

3. Go to **Backups** and that is where you find all the backed-up files.

If you wish to delete a backed-up file, select a file from the displayed list and tap Delete and Turn Off Backup.

iCloud Syncing

If this feature on your iPhone SE is on for a specific app, its information will be automatically stored in iCloud. To turn on this feature, go to Settings,tap on your name, and proceed to iCloud. Finally, tap on Show All and go to the particular app and turn it on.

Using Mac to Backup Your iPhone

The first step here is to connect your iPhone SE device to your computer with a cable.

1. Select Your **iPhone** in the **Finder sidebar** on your Mac

2. However, for **Finder** to be able to back up your iPhone, macOS 10.15 or any other updated version is needed. If you have earlier macOS versions, you should use **iTunes** to perform the backup.

3. Go to the **Finder** window and look at the top where you have to click **General.**

4. Click on **Backup all of your data on your iPhone to this Mac** prompt.

5. It is best that you encrypt backed-up data and safeguard it with a password. To do this, click **Encrypt local backup.**

6. Finally, click **Back Up Now.**

Note that it is possible for you to wirelessly connect your device to a computer by setting up syncing over Wi-Fi.

Backing Up iPhone Using Windows PC

You can also use a Windows PC to backup files on your iPhone SE. If you do not have macOS, you can alternatively use your Windows computer.

1. First, connect the iPhone to a Windows PC with a cable.

2. Open the **iTunes** app on your computer.

3. On the iTunes window, go to the top left and click on the **iPhone** icon.

4. Next, click **Summary.**

5. Go to **Back Up Now** and click on it.

6. You can encrypt your backups by selecting **Encrypt local backup,** and create a password.

You can also view the backups that are stored on your computer by choosing Edit, and proceed to Preferences. Then, click Devices. Backups that are encrypted should appear in the backups list with a lock icon next to each one of them. It is also possible to connect your iPhone SE to a Windows computer by setting up syncing over Wi-Fi.

Restore Information From a Backup

You can retrieve the backed-up information whenever you need it, be it when you are using a new device or the entire data has been wiped out.

1. To complete this task, you should connect your iPhone to the computer that you use for syncing.

2. Switch on **Wi-Fi Syncing.**

3. Go to your PC and open the **iTunes** app.

4. Go to the **iTunes** window and click the **Device** icon that is close to the top left.

5. Click **Summary.**

6. Now, click **Restore Backup.**

Note that if the backup is encrypted, iTunes will ask you to punch in your password before the restoration of files begins. Remember, information that is automatically backed up includes notes, text messages, contact favorites, call history, widget settings, sound settings, and more. Files like the **Saved Pictures** or **Camera Roll** are also under backup.

Unfortunately, media files that include videos, songs, and some pictures are not backed up. However, they can be restored by syncing with iTunes. Make sure that you disconnect your device from the computer by clicking the **Eject** button when the restoration is complete.

Chapter 8: Using Popular Apps

iPhone SE is a user-friendly device that has a **Maps** app that can guide and lead you to your intended destination with ease. The app shows you detailed information about bike lanes, buildings, crosswalks, and a street-level view that enables you to access the correct lanes as you get closer to complex interchanges. The smooth navigation functions make your travels or visits easier, especially in unfamiliar locations.

Directions for Driving

Make sure that you activate Siri on your device so that you can use voice commands while driving. Siri will respond out loud each time you give a command.

1. First, say **"Hey Siri,"** and then give out a command or question. In relation to driving, you can say "Hey Siri, give me directions to the gym."

2. When **Maps** shows you the destination, you can touch and hold any spot on the map.

3. Go to the **Directions** button and tap on it once.

4. Maps suggest routes for you and, once they appear, you can then switch to driving
directions. This only applies if your device's default mode of travel is not set on driving.

If you want to view the possible directions of a selected route, you should go to the **route card** and tap on the **estimated travel time.** The particular route will shift to the top of the card. Once this happens, you should tap the estimated time of travel once more. If you wish to share these directions with someone else, just scroll to the bottom end and tap **Share.**

Choosing a Future Time of Departure or Arrival

To get this done:

1. Go just below the directions list and tap **Now**.

2. Choose a preferred date and time of departure or arrival and tap **Done.**

Please note that, **Maps** can predict the state of traffic on a certain route and this affects the estimated time of travel that it shows you.

Adding the Intended Stops

It is possible to add a maximum of 14 stops along the route to the destination.

1. Go below **Directions** and tap **Add Stop.** You can make use of the search bar or results of recent searches to find and choose a place to stop.

2. Now, go to the search results and select the intended stopping places. You can also
go to the search result place card and tap **Add Stop.**

3. Another interesting feature of the Maps app is that you can zoom in as well as move
the map. This can be a business or landmark. You should go to the place card and tap **Add Stop.** Touching and holding a particular spot will highlight it with a pin. Go to the place card and tap **Add Stop** afterward.

4. If you want to view a selected stop, go to the **Directions list** and it will be listed

Switching a Point of Departure and Destination

To do this, follow these steps:

1. You can change the point of departure and destination on the Maps app. Go to the **Directions list.**

2. Touch and hold it to indicate your intended starting point.

3. Then, slide it just below the destination.

You can also select a new or different point of departure or destination. Go to the **Directions** list and tap either the starting point or destination. Use the recent search results or search field to find and choose a new location.

Using the App Store

The App Store allows you to access and enjoy different apps and games. You should just download and install the app or game from the App Store and you are good to go.

Open the App Store on Your iPhone

You can view available games and apps by going through **Apps, Today Games,** or **Arcade** tabs. You can alternatively look for a specific app or game by tapping the **Search** tab and typing in the name. In case you want to play a game tagged **"Arcade,"** you can kindly subscribe to **Apple Arcade** to access it.

Tap the **Get** or **Price** button. If the **Open** button appears on your screen in place of the **Price** or **Get** button, the game or app is already purchased or downloaded.

Please note that, if you visit the App Store and you find an app or game that has a Get button in place of a price, it is free. Remember, you will not get any charges for free app downloads. However, certain free apps have in-app purchases or subscriptions that you can pay for. Such in-app purchases or subscriptions give you more content and features for particular apps and games.

How to Install Apps on iPhone SE

1. Start by opening the **App Store** and select **Search.**

2. Go to the search bar, enter the name of the app, and tap **Search.**

3. Go to the selected app and tap **Get.**

4. Two options will show up are **Use Existing Apple ID** and **Create New Apple ID.** Tap **Use Existing Apple ID.**

5. Type in your Apple ID username and password. Then, tap **Ok.**

You may need to get an Apple ID password before getting access to app downloads and installation.

SSID: This refers to a character sequence that is related to a specific Wi-Fi Network.

Text message: This is a written communication that is electronically exchanged between senders and receivers over mobile phones.

Touch-ID: This is a security-enhancing, personal identification technology that uses fingerprints for authentication and access to apps and devices.

Voicemail: This describes a voice message that is electronically stored so that it can be
retrieved by the receiver, especially after a voice call that didn't go through.

Wi-Fi: This refers to a networking technology where radio waves are used to provide internet access.

Avoiding Highways or Tolls

To enable this option, you look just below the **Directions list** and tap the option **Avoid.** Choose the option that you want to avoid, and tap **Apply.** After confirming all the settings, tap **Go** to activate the route that you want. The Maps app will start leading you by making
turn-by-turn directions as you travel toward your destination.

You do not have to worry about keeping your iPhone screen on when **Driving Focus** is on. Maps will remain on screen and continue speaking directions even if you start using or opening other apps. If you want to switch back to Maps from another app, go to the **Directions banner** that is at the top screen and tap it once. You can also tap the **navigation indicator** on the status bar.

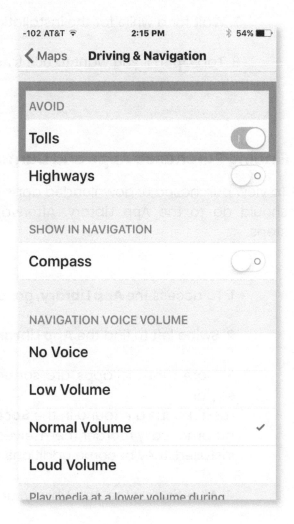

Display or Hide the Compass Speed limit

To get this done:

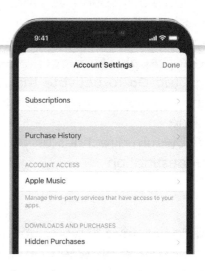

1. Open **Settings** and go to **Maps.**

2. Go below **Directions** and tap **Driving.**

3. Now, turn the speed limit or campus on or off.

Ending Driving Directions Before Getting to the Destination

Ending driving directions can be easily done through Siri. You can say, "Hey Siri, cancel or stop navigating." It is also possible to stop navigating without using Siri. Just tap on the card that is at the lower part of the device's screen. The last step is to tap the End Route prompt.

6. Tap **Install** and select **Done.**

7. Wait for a while for the installation to finish.

8. Tap **Open** if you want to use the app immediately.

Finding Purchased Apps and Games

To view purchased or downloaded apps and games, you should go to the App Library. Afterward, follow these steps:

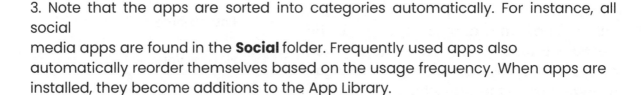

1. To access the **App Library,** go to the **Home Screen.**

2. Swipe left to find the **App Library.**

3. Note that the apps are sorted into categories automatically. For instance, all social
media apps are found in the **Social** folder. Frequently used apps also
automatically reorder themselves based on the usage frequency. When apps are installed, they become additions to the App Library.

4. After finding the App Library, go to the search field and type in the app's name.

Deleting a Downloaded App From the iPhone SE Device

If you no longer need an app that you already downloaded, you just have to delete it and free up the space in your device.

1. Select **App Library** and search for the app.

2. Go to the unwanted app, tap and hold its icon.

3. The app will highlight itself, and then tap **Delete App.**

4. To confirm this action, tap **Delete** again.

Note that, if the App Store is not showing up on your device, the parental control feature might be turned on. You should adjust the **iTunes and App Store Purchases settings** and go to **Installing Apps.** Then, tap **Allow** and the App Store will reappear. If you cannot still find the App Store, you should swipe to look for it.

Using Music and Podcasts

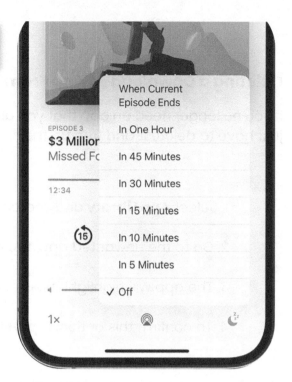

iTunes is the most decorated source of music known to iPhone users. You can transfer music from an Android phone or computer to your iPhone SE device to add to your entertainment basket. This can also be done without the services of iTunes.

Adding Music From iTunes to iPhone SE

iTunes was developed by Apple to make it easy for users to manage media files. It also helps users to sync stored files to iOS devices. If you want to copy music from a computer to your iPhone SE, you should add the respective songs to the iTunes library and sync them to your iPhone.

1. The first step is to download and install the recent version of iTunes on your PC.

2. Connect your iPhone device to the computer. iTunes usually launches itself automatically, but if it does not, you can open it yourself.

3. On the first connection attempt, a window shows up on your PC and you should confirm the process by clicking **Continue.** This way you will be allowing iTunes to read the data on your iPhone. Now, tap Trust.

4. On your PC, click the device icon and proceed to **Summary.** Uncheck the option, **"Automatically sync when this iPhone is connected,"** and check the **"Manually manage music and videos,"** option.

5. To confirm this action, click **Apply.**

6. Select the **File** option and click **Add File to Library** to add the selected music that you intend to transfer to your iPhone to iTunes.

7. Now, open **Music** and check **Sync Music.**

8. Select the option to sync the entire music library, selected artists, genres, and playlists.

9. Then, click **Apply** to begin syncing music from iTunes to your device.

It is important to note that you cannot sync music files from different libraries of iTunes. Your device can only be paired with one computer.

Transferring Music From PC to Your iPhone SE Without Using iTunes

You can use Dropbox, Media Monkey, or FoneTool to execute the music transfer. **FoneTool** is one of the best iPhone data transfer and backup tools that you can use on your Windows PC. This tool was developed with its main objective focused on data security for at least 10 years. It is also used to transfer music, videos, and photos between your iPhone and PC.

1. The first step is to ensure that your computer has FoneTool installed. Use a USB cable to connect your iPhone to your PC.

2. Open **FoneTool,** and click **PC to iPhone.**

3. Highlight the songs that you wish to transfer. Then, drag and drop them. You can browse the files in the computer and select the songs you want by clicking the plus (+).

4. The final step is to click **Start Transfer** to copy music to your iPhone SE.

Playing Music on iPhone SE

Follow these steps:

1. Tap on the music player icon and select **Playlists** to create a playlist.

2. Tap New Playlist and go to the input field to name the playlist.

3. Press Add Music and select the music files from the respective category.

4. Tap Done and proceed by tapping on Done again.

5. Go to the playlist or category, and tap on the audio file that you need.

6. Tap on the respective audio file and it will start playing.

7. To go to the next file, tap the arrow right.

8. Double-tap the arrow left to play the previous audio.

9. Tap the shuffle icon that is just below the name of the audio file to turn it on or off.

10. Tapping the repeat icon, located to the right of the shuffle icon, turns this function on or off.

11. To exit the App, press the home key.

Finding Podcasts on iPhone

The podcasts app is used to find shows about news, politics, science, comedy, and many more. You can create your library by following the shows that you like. This makes it easy for you to listen while offline, as well as receive notifications on new developments and episodes on particular shows.

Shows may also have paid subscription offers that enable you to access exclusive shows, episodes without ads, new releases, and more. To find podcasts, you should search for a particular topic, title, or person.

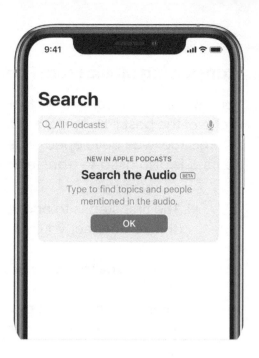

1. On the **Podcasts** app, go to the bottom right and tap **Search.**

2. Enter the details of what you are searching for in the search bar.

You can also discover newly released shows by going to the bottom of your screen and tapping **Browse.** This way, you can view **New and Noteworthy, featured shows,** as well as the **Apple editorial collections.** You can browse **Top Charts** by tapping Search. As you view and listen to selected episodes, some personalized recommendations pop up on the **"Listen Now"** screen, making it easier for you to discover the next show to consider.

You can add shows by URL by tapping **Browse.** Then, tap **Follow a Show by URL.** However, the URL should be in RSS format.

How to View Shared Podcasts

A friend or loved one can share shows with you in **Messages.** However, the friends have to be in your contacts for you to use this feature.

1. You can find the shared details in **Shared with you Podcasts.** However, you should go to **Settings** and make sure that **Podcasts** are turned on.

2. After opening **Settings,** proceed to **Messages.**

3. Go to Shared with You.

4. To access the shared **Podcasts,** you should just tap **Listen Now** and scroll to **Shared With You.**

Chapter 9: Accessibility Features

As a senior citizen, you may find difficulties in using your phone. The iPhone SE is great in that it allows you to use its accessibility features to your advantage. We will explain more about how to use the voiceover, magnifier, visual, and hearing features.

In case you have impaired vision or cognitive difficulty, you may want to use the accessibility features to ease the use of your device. There are also features to help you improve your hearing if you have problems.

How to Use Accessibility Features

To start using the accessibility features, choose the **Settings** app from the home screen. Afterward, go to **General,** then choose **Accessibility.** From here, you can then access the various features which include. Let's start our discussion with the voiceover feature.

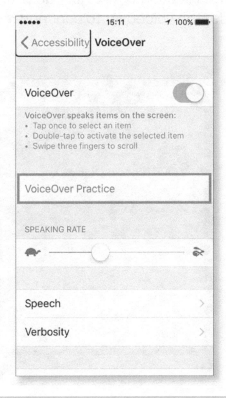

Voiceover

The voiceover option helps to read everything that is written on your screen. This can be done even when you are not looking at the device. The voiceover is remarkable because it
can give you distinct descriptions of what is happening on your iPhone's screen, be it which app your finger is pointing at, battery level, or who is calling you. With the voiceover feature, you can tune the pitch and speaking rate according to your preference. In addition, the voiceover is able to inform you when the display orientation changes toportrait or landscape. In case your screen has locked or dimmed, voiceover lets you know.How remarkable!

Turning on Voiceover

There are various ways to use the voiceover accessibility feature. For example, you can ask Siri to switch on the voiceover feature. Alternatively, you can find **Accessibility** by pressing Settings. Under the **Settings** option, tap on **Accessibility.** Afterward, tap on the **Voiceover** option to switch it on.

Upon switching on the Voiceover option, you can press the **Home** button to go back to your initial screen. From here, you can tap any icon of choice and the voiceover feature will read out whatever is shown on your screen. You can also swipe to the right or left in order to find an icon of choice. As you swipe, the voiceover feature will read out any item that appears on the screen. Another way to hear your voiceover reading out the contents of your screen is to drag your finger on it. As you drag your finger and point out the icons, the voiceover will read it out.

Activating or Opening an App Using Voiceover

To open or activate a particular app, button, or link on your iPhone SE, simply double tap on it. For instance, if you want to send a text message, just double-tap on the **Messages** icon. From there, you can choose to start a conversation with someone or you can continue with one.

If you wish your voiceover to pause while reading a certain section of text, just do a single tap using two fingers. Simply tap again with two fingers for the voiceover to continue reading.

Magnifier

It is possible to magnify items using the camera of your iPhone. By using the **Magnifier** app, you can use your iPhone as a magnifying glass that allows you to zoom in on text or objects near you. The magnifier app makes use of your iPhone's camera to make them appear large so that you can view them with ease. You can switch on the flashlight and increase the zoom level so that text and objects are better displayed. It is also possible for you to play around with the brightness of the image, apply color filters, as well as increase the contrast. You could also freeze the frames in order to review them.

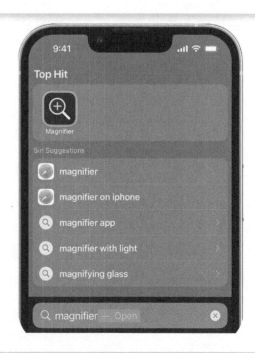

Setting Up the Magnifier App on Your iPhone

To set up the **Magnifier** app using your iPhone SE, go ahead and tap **Settings,** then **Accessibility.** Afterward, press the **Accessibility Shortcut** before tapping on **Magnifier.** After doing this set up, you can triple-tap your iPhone to use it as a magnifier and other options

If you would like to add Magnifier through the Control Center, tap on your iPhone **Settings** app and go down until you find the **Control Center** option and tap. The control center setup will display various controls at the screen's top side. It is possible for you to add more controls at the bottom if you like.

As you continue to go down, you are more likely to find the magnifier option. Once you do, press the green plus (+) sign icon that is beside it so that the magnifier will appear as one of your control center options.

Hearing and Visual Accessibility Features

Due to old age or other reasons, you may be experiencing problems with your vision and hearing. The iPhone SE offers you a solution through its hearing and visual accessibility features. Some of these include hearing aids, video subtitles, visual alerts, FaceTime video calls, and headphone accommodations. Let's zoom in on some of these features:

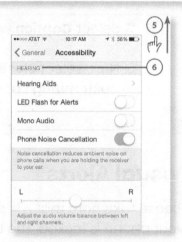

Hearing Aids

With this feature, you can hear various audio or phone calls more clearly. This is made possible by using **Made for iPhone** hearing aids, which you can simply pair with your device. You will have to control the feature using your iPhone.

1. To pair your hearing device, switch on your **Bluetooth** in Settings and open the battery doors of your hearing device.

2. On your iPhone SE tap on Settings, then Accessibility. Afterward, select **Hearing** and **choose Hearing Devices**. Shut the battery doors of your hearing device so that your iPhone searches for the hearing device.

3. Tap on the name of your hearing device as it appears under the **MFi hearing devices**. Once you see the tapping request on the screen, tap **pair.**

4. Please note that the pairing process may take up to a minute. From here, you can commence using your hearing device when you see it under the MFi Hearing Devices option that has a checkmark.

Video Subtitles

To effect a language of choice or subtitles while watching a video, slightly press the screen so that you can open the playback controls. Tap on the More controls option, and select Subtitles or Languages. Afterward, pick the audio language or subtitles that you desire.

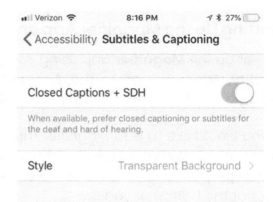

In a case where you want to turn on **SDH** or **Closed Captioning** by default, follow these steps:

1. Open Settings and select **Accessibility.**

2. Select **Captioning and Subtitles** under the **Hearing** option.

3. Next, select **Closed Captions Plus SDH** in order to switch it on. If you are interested in customizing captions and subtitles, select **Style** then choose an option.

Visual Alerts

Please take note that it is possible for you to receive a visual alert when your phone is locked. The LED flash on your iPhone SE can blink, thereby signaling that some form of communication has occurred. This is very helpful because it helps you not to miss a notification when your device is locked.

If you are interested in turning on your **Visual Alert,** go to the **Settings** app and tap **Accessibility** before tapping on **Audio/Visual.** Afterward, switch on **LED Flash for Alerts.**

Headphone Accommodations

Another interesting feature of the iPhone SE is the headphone accommodations. This allows you to customize your headphone audio settings so that you can amplify and change particular frequencies to your desired hearing needs.

1. To effect headphone accommodation, tap on **Settings, Accessibility, Audio/Visual,** and **Headphone Accommodations.**

2. Afterward, switch on **Headphone Accommodations.** Then, select how you want to use your custom audio settings.

Chapter 10: Troubleshooting Common Issues

iPhones unquestionably excel when they exhibit smooth and efficient performance. That does not mean, though, that Apple's much-discussed smartphone has not seen its fair share of problems. However, some helpful hints and techniques might address the frequent issues that arise with the iPhone from time to time. For instance, the iPhone's "black screen of death" can occur when the Apple logo does not appear in specific circumstances. You should attempt restarting your iPhone as a first step in solving this issue, which could be brought on by a failed upgrade, hardware ware issue, or jailbreak. or might have to choose a hard reset (factory reset) for your iPhone. Getting assistance from experts if you fail to rectify a problem on your iPhone is also a great idea. This chapter will elaborate on what you should do when your iPhone is not charging, apps are not working well, and has Wi-Fi or cellular connectivity problems.

iPhone SE Won't Turn On or Charge

If your iPhone charges up to 80%, there is no need for you to worry even if it doesn't continue. The item, which was referred to as optimized battery charging in recent years in iOS 13, is what can make this possible. You can tell it is the cable if your iPhone charges with one but not another. You also can recognize that the problem is your phone when the cable charges other individuals phones except for yours. If you discover that your phone is now charging, anything you recently adjusted was the issue. Some of the steps you should take when your cell phone has charging problems are as follows:

Switch Your iPhone Off and On Again

Restarting the system and checking to see whether that resolves the issue is always helpful when debugging a problem. You have to restart your phone to see if there is still enough power left before attempting to charge it once more.

Be Sure That Your iPhone is Not Charging

Before you proceed, check if your cellphone is not charging. Check the phone's display after connecting it to whatever method you normally use to charge it. If your battery has run out of power, charge it for approximately two hours and thirty minutes. A lightning bolt should be next to or inside the battery icon in the upper right corner of the iPhone's lock screen. If there is no lightning strike nearby, your iPhone will not charge.

Try Not to Charge Your iPhone Wirelessly

If you are using a wireless charging case, take it off and use a lightning cable to connect the phone to a power source. Once more, make sure it is charging. If the iPhone charges, this means that the wireless charging system is faulty. You may need to replace your wireless charging cover or take your phone to an Apple store for repair; but in the meanwhile, you can continue to charge it conventionally using wires.

Check Your iPhone's Lightning Port

If your phone isn't charging properly, troubleshoot the lightning port. After all, we routinely stuff our phones into lint and dust-filled pockets, wallets, and other locations, usually with the port end first. You can gently remove whatever you find after taking a close look using a toothpick, a pointed instrument, or any other suitable object. You can also use a blower to quickly blow the port and recharge the phone once more.

Inspect Your Cable

You have undoubtedly seen a damaged or frayed cable if you've had an iPhone long enough. The rubberized outside sheath cracks due to continuous bending, thereby exposing the wires. Throw away your cable and buy a new one if this is the case. Quite often, lightning cables are frequently misused, and issues are not always visible to the human eye. Sometimes, wires that are still encased in the sheath can break. Cheap thirdparty lightning cables were known to stop functioning on their own, frequently as a result of a broken power regulation chip within the cable.

The simplest approach to test your lightning cable is to start trying another one, preferably a completely authorized one from Apple that is brand-new. There is no decent way to visually observe all this.

Examine Where Your iPhone Is Plugged In

Examine your power source as part of the long checklist for possible issues. When you are charging your Apple phone via a USB port attached to a computer, keep in mind that your computer should be fully awake. In other words, it should not be in sleep mode. For instance, if the USB port you had been using failed, try a different one. You have to connect it directly to a USB port on your computer.

If it still does not work, try using an AC adapter similar to the one that comes with your iPhone to connect it directly to a power socket. If you have been plugging it into an AC adapter every time, try a different one. You can use the one that comes with an iPad or borrow one from your friend.

Look for Software Updates

If you are not running the most recent version of iOS, your phone might not charge. Software updates may not seem important when your phone is functioning normally, but they help you avoid many problems and even improve performance. To check if your phone needs to be updated, you can click on your **settings.** Go and select **Software Updates** under **General.** After doing that, select **Install now.** After the update has been installed, restart your phone.

If neither of these troubleshooting steps helps your phone function again, there is unquestionably a problem with the iPhone. You should call Apple or go to an Apple retail outlet for assistance.

Apps Are Crashing or Not Working

The tasks on your iPhone are completed using apps, whether they are third-party or native to Apple. It is possible for a few apps to occasionally cease operating on your iPhone. They might not launch or simply remain frozen on the loading screen. Some apps might launch occasionally, but close or crash right away. There are a few steps you should take to rectify such issues and we will explore them in this section.

Force or Quit the IOS App

This is the initial solution for crashing, unresponsive, and misbehaving apps. To stop an app immediately, do the following:

1. On an iPhone with Face ID, scroll up from the bottom of the screen while holding to get the **App Switcher.**

2. Double-press the **Home** button if your iPhone has one.

3. To force stop a non-functioning program, drag its card up.

4. Open the app again and check to see whether it still works after 15 seconds.

Restart Your Phone

One of the go-to solutions for practically any minor issue, including app failure, is to turn off your iPhone and then switch it on again. Use the physical buttons on your iPhone to restart it, or select **General Shut Down** under **Settings**. Turn on your iPhone after a minute and launch the app that wasn't functioning before. It probably will function after this reboot.

Update Your Apps

If you don't update some apps, they can quit functioning. This is normally observed with carrier apps that include Vodafone, bank apps, and others. Consider updating to the newest version if the app suddenly stops functioning. Follow these steps:

1. Long-press the **App Store** icon on the iPhone home screen or **App Library**, and select **Updates.**

2. The page should load. To refresh the list of available app updates, pull down the page.

3. Next to an app, select **Update.** You could also select **Update All**

You can also engage in other options like contacting the app developer, checking the app restrictions, deleting and installing the apps, or resetting iPhone settings.

Wi-Fi or Cellular Connectivity Issues

Your iPhone can show that it is connected to Wi-Fi when there is a proper network. Sometimes, it can show a "no internet connection" message where there is no network. This notification typically shows when your iPhone is too far from the Wi-Fi router to make a reliable connection, which is a common cause. See whether the notice disappears by getting your phone close to the Wi-Fi router. If the connectivity problem persists, be sure to restart your iPhone and carry out some of the methods that are described below.

Switch Your Wi-Fi Off and On

When your iPhone is not connecting to the internet, the first thing to do is to turn the **WiFi** off and then back on. This provides your iPhone with an additional opportunity to connect to your Wi-Fi network, which can fix a minor software issue. Tap Wi-Fi after opening **Settings.** Tap the Wi-Fi switch at the top of the menu after that. After a brief delay, turn on **Wi-Fi** once more.

Forget the Wi-Fi Connection

Connectivity problems can be resolved by forgetting the **Wi-Fi** connection on your iPhone and **setting** it up from scratch. Your iPhone remembers details about the network and how to connect to it when you first connect to a **Wi-Fi** network. Your iPhone may not be able to connect to the internet or may display "No Internet Connection" if a step in that connection procedure has changed.

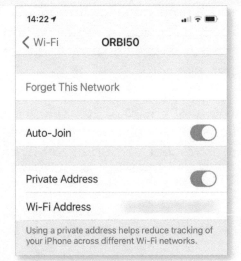

Before you proceed with this troubleshooting step, be sure to write down your Wi-Fi password. When you re-join the network, you will need to input it again. Tap **Wi-Fi** after opening **Settings.** Then, click **Forget This Network** by tapping the **information** button next to your Wi-Fi network.

Restart Your Router

Your Wi-Fi router may occasionally be at fault when your internet connection is down. Your router might need to be restarted. First, remove your router's plug from the wall. After a brief delay, plug it back in. Your router will restart and begin reconnecting. This can take a while.

The other option is to check your VPN settings because it is possible that they could hinder your phone from connecting to Wi-Fi. Let's look at the other factors that are associated with a cellular connection.

Troubleshoot on Cellular Data

Switching the cellular data on and off might occasionally resolve small connectivity issues. To do this, click **Settings,** then click **Cellular,** and the switch adjacent to cellular data should then be turned off. After a few minutes, turn it back on.

Removing and Reinstalling Your SIM Card

Your iPhone connects to your carrier's cellular network using a SIM card. Connectivity issues can be resolved by removing and reinserting the SIM card. On the side of your iPhone, there is a tray where you may find your **SIM card.** Try connecting to the internet after reinstalling your SIM card

You might need to do a deeper reset on your iPhone if, after following the previous instructions, it still won't connect to the internet. Before you do, ensure your iPhone is running the most recent version of iOS by going to your **Settings, General,** and then   If a software update is available, select Download and Install.

Conclusion

Having gone through this book, you might have realized how easy using your iPhone is. We have covered the basics, ranging from unboxing your gadget to troubleshooting issues that might arise as you use your phone. Information on how to connect to the internet was unleashed in this book. We also highlighted how you can carry out important tasks that are done using the Internet, including emailing and FaceTime calling. Even the steps for sending text messages and making direct voice calls were elaborated on.

Your iPhone is a great tool for entertainment, and procedures on how to keep yourself occupied using this gadget were highlighted in this book. You can make memories by taking photos with your phone using the steps that are described herein. You can even download music and keep yourself entertained. There is no way you will ever get lost on the way to your intended destination when you can use the Maps app. More interestingly, most of the tasks are even easier to complete when you know how to use Siri as you do now. With Siri, you can make calls and do many other tasks without having to go through too many clicks, unless you prefer to do so.

As you use your iPhone, be sure to be on the lookout for any discrepancies so that you can address them at an early stage. Avoid procrastinating when it comes to dealing with issues
that arise on your phone. Doing so helps to make sure that minor issues do not escalate into bigger problems that might cost you a lot of money and time to solve. In this book,we highlighted some common problems that you might face as you enjoy your iPhone SE, along with some troubleshooting suggestions.

This book has given you the basics that you need to get started with using your iPhone SE. If you desire to know your iPhone even better and get the best out of it, you can search for what you need on the internet. You might even get information from online conversations with people who own iPhone SE or those who once had this gadget before. Such conversations are great when you are looking for a way to deal with specific problems on your iPhone SE, especially those that have not been touched on in this book.

It is my sincere desire that you get the best out of your iPhone SE using the foundation that has been laid out using this guide.

Glossary

Apple Pay: This is a platform that allows you to make contactless purchases that are secure using, say, Apple Card or Apple Cash.

Application: This refers to software that is used to perform specific tasks on your phone.

Application: This refers to software that is used to perform specific tasks on your phone.

Artificial Intelligence: This describes the scenario where computer systems and applications are designed to perform tasks that are normally completed through human intelligence. Good examples of such tasks include decision-making and voice recognition.

Backup: This refers to a copy of stored data, meant to be a replacement in the event that the original information is damaged or lost.

Contacts: This describes the list of saved phone numbers in your iPhone.

Email: This is the distribution of electronic messages between a sender and one or more recipients over the Internet.

Siri: This is a virtual assistant that utilizes voice recognition technology.
Software: This refers to information, instructions, or programs that make it possible for computers to complete particular tasks.

Face-ID: This describes a face r hat allows users to engage in video calls in real-time.

HEIF: This is a compression format that allows smaller photo sizes of high quality and definition to be created.

Internet: This is a system that is made up of interconnected computer networks that enhance communication and sharing of information between users.

iCloud: This is a storage facility for your notes, photos, passwords, or files, which is automatically updated across all devices that belong to you.

iTunes: This refers to an application that is used for organizing, downloading, and playing music and videos, among other things.

LAN: This refers to a group of computers within a particular location, linked to create a network.

PNG: This describes a compression file format that is lossless.

References

The best secure phone to phone transfer solution. (n.d.). Mobiletrans.

https://mobiletrans.wondershare.com

Adobe.

(2019). Creative, marketing and document management solutions.

Adobe.

https://www.adobe.com

Apple.

(2019, July 10). If Siri or "Hey Siri" isn't working. Apple Support.

https://support.apple.com/en-us/HT207489

Apple iPhone SE (1st Gen): Set up voicemail. (n.d.). AT&T.

https://www.att.com/device⊠support/article/wireless/KM1263698/Apple/iPhoneSE/

Apple iPhone SE (2nd Gen): Send and receive messages. (n.d.). AT&T.

https://www.att.com/device⊠support/article/wireless/KM1405416/Apple/iPhoneSE2ndGen

Apple iPhone SE (2020) : Write and send text messages. (

n.d.). Vodafone

Australia.

https://devices.vodafone.com.au/apple/iphone-se-2020-ios-13-

4/messaging/write-and-send-text-messages/

Apple Support. (n.d.). Change Siri settings on iPhone. Apple Support.

https://support.apple.com/en-za/guide/iphone/iphc28624b81/ios

Apple Support. (n.d.-b). Use accessibility features with Siri on iPhone. Apple

Support.

https://support.apple.com/en⊠za/guide/iphone/iphaff1d606/16.0/ios/16.0

References

Apple Support. (2022, November 8). Manage and delete contacts on your iPhone or iPad. Apple Support.

https://support.apple.com/en-gb/HT207207

AT&T. (n.d.). Apple iPhone SE (2nd Gen): Set up email. AT&T.

https://www.att.com/device⊠support/article/wireless/KM1274282/Apple/iPhoneSE2ndGen

Bryant, M. (2020, January 17). Ultimate guide to manage contacts on your iPhone. GroovyPost.

https://www.groovypost.com/howto/ultimate-guide-to⊠manage-contacts-on-your-iphone/

Chan, C., & Keller, J. (2022, March 14). How to make a FaceTime call on iPhone, iPad, or Mac. IMore.

https://www.imore.com/how-place-facetime-call-your⊠iphone

Coleman, S. (2023, February 28). How to use Apple Maps: A step-by-step guide for seniors. Senior Living.

https://www.seniorliving.org/tech/how-to-use-apple⊠maps/

Cook, I. (2022, May 5). How to check voicemail on iPhone SE/6s/6/5s/5c/5/4s/4/3GS. ISkysoft.

https://www.iskysoft.com/article/check⊠voicemail-on-iphone.html

Das, T. (2023, January 4). How to update iPhone without Wi-Fi: 5 best methods in 2023. Technipages.

https://www.technipages.com/how-to-update-iphone⊠without-wi-fi/

GCF Global. (2018, July). iPhone basics: Adding and managing contacts. GCF Global.

https://edu.gcfglobal.org/en/iphonebasics/adding-and-managing⊠contacts/1

References

Apple Support. (2022, November 8). Manage and delete contacts on your iPhone or iPad. Apple Support.

https://support.apple.com/en-gb/HT207207

AT&T. (n.d.). Apple iPhone SE (2nd Gen): Set up email. AT&T.

https://www.att.com/device⊠support/article/wireless/KM1274282/Apple/iPhoneSE2ndGen

Bryant, M. (2020, January 17). Ultimate guide to manage contacts on your iPhone. GroovyPost.

https://www.groovypost.com/howto/ultimate-guide-to⊠manage-contacts-on-your-iphone/

Chan, C., & Keller, J. (2022, March 14). How to make a FaceTime call on iPhone, iPad, or Mac. IMore.

https://www.imore.com/how-place-facetime-call-your⊠iphone

Coleman, S. (2023, February 28). How to use Apple Maps: A step-by-step guide for seniors. Senior Living.

https://www.seniorliving.org/tech/how-to-use-apple⊠maps/

Cook, I. (2022, May 5). How to check voicemail on iPhone SE/6s/6/5s/5c/5/4s/4/3GS. ISkysoft.

https://www.iskysoft.com/article/check⊠voicemail-on-iphone.html

Das, T. (2023, January 4). How to update iPhone without Wi-Fi: 5 best methods in 2023. Technipages.

https://www.technipages.com/how-to-update-iphone⊠without-wi-fi/

GCF Global. (2018, July). iPhone basics: Adding and managing contacts. GCF Global.

https://edu.gcfglobal.org/en/iphonebasics/adding-and-managing⊠contacts/1

Made in United States
Cleveland, OH
31 October 2024

10394285R00044